B

FLORENCE &
TUSCANY

*The Essential Guide to the Land of the
Renaissance and Rolling Hills*

VESNA NESKOW

MAPS BY DAVID LINDROTH INC.

ILLUSTRATED BY
KERREN BARBAS STECKLER

PETER PAUPER PRESS, INC.
WHITE PLAINS, NEW YORK

TO PAUL AND JACKIE,
WHO KNOW HOW TO SAVOR GREAT FOOD,
FINE WINE, AND THE GOOD LIFE

The publisher has made every effort to ensure that the content of this book was current at time of publication. It's always best, however, to confirm information before making final travel plans, since telephone numbers, Web sites, prices, hours of operation, and other facts are always subject to change. The publisher cannot accept responsibility for any consequences arising from the use of this book. We value your feedback and suggestions. Please write to: Editors, Peter Pauper Press, Inc., 202 Mamaroneck Avenue, Suite 400, White Plains, New York 10601-5376.

Editors: Mara Conlon and Suzanne Schwalb
Proofreader: JCommunications, LLC

Cover image (back cover and front inset) and p. 255: © pandapaw

Sunflowers (cover background): © Anthony Ricci

Illustrations copyright © 2011 Kerren Barbas Steckler
Florence transportation map © 2011 ATAF SpA
Used with permission.
Neighborhood maps © 2011 David Lindroth Inc.

Designed by Heather Zschock

Visit us at www.peterpauper.com

THE LITTLE
BLACK BOOK OF

FLORENCE
& TUSCANY

CONTENTS

INTRODUCTION

The promise of enchantment that a trip to Tuscany brings stems from the region's unique blend of breathtaking landscapes, medieval towns, Renaissance art and architecture, rich culinary traditions, cultural events, and the pleasures of a restful countryside. From majestic mountains to brimming seas, from rolling hills to fertile valleys, from lush woods to aromatic vineyards, Tuscany offers a widely varied experience of beauty. Its rich history of international influence and regional rivalries has left a vibrant imprint on the cities and towns of the region. Florence, one of the greatest repositories of art masterpieces in the world, is a veritable treasure trove of Renaissance art and architecture. Its age-old rival Siena holds its own unforgettable charms while smaller but equally historic towns, such as Pisa, Lucca, Arezzo, and Cortona, exude a unique magic and individuality. Stunning medieval towns—Montepulciano, Montalcino, and San Gimignano among them—with their fortified walls and hilltop views, recall earlier eras of internecine wars for power just as the southern expanses of the Maremma, with its villages characteristically strewn with Etruscan ruins, remind one that Tuscany's past is varied and prehistoric. Among the pleasures of the region not to be missed are the famous cuisine, rich in ingredients produced locally, and equally renowned wines. Most important, as you travel through this evocative cornucopia, take your time. Measure your steps not by the number of places you see but by the depth of the experience.

HOW TO USE THIS GUIDE

This guidebook is divided into two sections: Florence and Tuscany. In **Part I: Florence**, each chapter covers an area of Florence and provides a map for that neighborhood. Each chapter in **Part II: Tuscany** surveys a part of the region and includes major towns, a regional map of the area, and small maps of the main towns, where appropriate.

Places mentioned in the text are identifiable by color. **Red** indicates **Places to See** (landmarks, arts & entertainment). **Blue** indicates **Places to Eat & Drink** (restaurants, cafés, bars, and nightlife). **Orange** indicates **Where to Shop**. **Green** indicates **Where to Stay**. For Florence, Lucca, Pisa, Siena, and Arezzo, the places correspond to color-coded numbers that appear on the maps. Some shops and restaurants are closed in July and August, so check before going. Each place mentioned is followed by its address, local telephone number, and, where available, Web site and hours of operation.

Here are our keys for restaurant and hotel costs:

Restaurants
Cost of an appetizer and main course without drinks

(€)	Up to €20
(€€)	€20–€40
(€€€)	€40–€60
(€€€€)	€60 and up

Hotels

Cost per room per night

(€)	Up to €100
(€€)	€100–€200
(€€€)	€200–€400
(€€€€)	€400 and up

Abbreviations

P.za	Square
SMN	Santa Maria Novella Train Station

BEST TIME TO VISIT

The best time of year to visit Tuscany is spring and autumn. Florence is stiflingly hot in July and August and swarming with mosquitoes. But it's the swarming tourists that make San Gimignano unbearable in summer.

ALL ABOUT MONEY

Money Changing

The currency in Italy is euros (€). Most places accept credit cards. For cash withdrawals in euros, ATMs *(bancomat)* offer good exchange rates. (Contact your bank before leaving home to determine if your PIN is valid internationally.) Exchange rates for cash or traveler's checks are best in banks (usually open M–F 8:30AM–1:30PM, 2:45PM–3:45PM), bad at the many independent exchange bureaus *(cambios)*, and worst at hotels and shops.

Tipping

Most restaurants add a service charge *(coperto)*, but an additional 5% to 10% is appropriate. At less fancy places €1 to €5 is OK. Don't look to the locals: foreigners should tip more. For drinks at bar counters, leave small change. For taxis, round up the fare. Leave chambermaids €1 to €2 per day; bellboys, €1 per bag; the concierge, €2 to €3. Theater ushers are tipped at least 50 euro-cents *(centesimi)*.

euro-Sense

Decimal points and commas are reversed from the U.S. system. So euros are separated from euro-cents *(centesimi)* by a comma, and hundreds are separated from thousands by a period (e.g., €2.425,50).

GETTING AROUND

Getting to & from the Airport

With so few flights into Tuscan airports, you might fly to Rome or Milan and take a connecting flight to one of the smaller airports, or take a train to Florence's Santa Maria Novella (SMN) train station or to the Pisa Centrale train station.

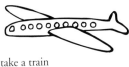

From Florence's **Amerigo Vespucci Airport** *(055-306.1300, www.aeroporto.firenze.it; hours: 5:30AM–11PM)*, also known as **Peretola**, the Volainbus goes to the **SITA** coach station *(Via Santa Caterina da Siena 15, SMN,*

800-373.760, *www.sitabus.it; hours: 6AM–11:30PM)* every half hour and costs €4. You can buy tickets on the bus. Taxis take about 20 to 30 minutes and cost about €16 (extra for luggage, at night, on Sundays and holidays).

From Pisa's **Galileo Galilei Airport** *(050-849.300, www.pisa-airport.com)*, **CPT** Bus 5 goes to Pisa Centrale every 10 minutes, where the last train to Florence is around 11:30PM. Pisa's Airport and Florence's SMN railway station are connected by six trains a day. Buy your ticket at the desk next to arrivals at the main terminal. Taxis from Galileo Airport to Pisa cost about €8. Returning trains begin to leave Florence from SMN for Pisa's airport at 6:30AM. Or take a train to Pisa Centrale, changing to the airport train there (usually Platform 14, via the underpass).

The **Terravision** bus *(050-260.80, www.terravision.eu/ florence-pisa.html)* connects Pisa's airport (outside arrivals) and Florence's SMN (main steps). Buy tickets at the Terravision kiosk (Pisa airport), Omega Viaggi (Florence, SMN), various hotels and travel agencies, or online or by phone (€10 one way; €16 round trip).

For online train tickets, go to *www.trenitalia.com*. Be sure to stamp your ticket and any supplements in the yellow machines on the platform.

Bus Tickets & Passes

City buses in Florence (ATAF), Pisa (CPT), and Siena (TRAIN) are bright orange and run until at least 9:30PM, longer in Florence. There is no subway in Florence, but ATAF covers most areas and most buses go to the SMN train station.

Tickets are sold at newsstands, bars, or *tabacchi*. Prices and length of validity vary from city to city (in Florence they cost €1.20, or €2 onboard bus, per trip and are valid one hour after machine validation). They must be stamped in the machine inside the bus. For bus routes and schedules, go to a tourist office or the ATAF office by the SMN train station in Florence *(Pza della Stazione, 800-424.500; hours: M–F 7:30AM–7:30PM, Sa 7:30AM–1:30PM, closed Sundays & holidays)*. Multi-day and student passes are also available at ATAF, TRAIN, and their affiliates.

ATAF: Piazza della Stazione, Florence, 800-424.500, *www.ataf.net*

CPT: Piazza Sant'Antonio 1, Pisa, 800-012.773 or 050-884.111, *www.cpt.pisa.it*

TRAIN: Piazza Antonio Gramsci, Siena, 0577-204.328, *www.trainspa.it*

Most buses in Pisa stop at the train station and Piazza Vittorio Emanuele II; in Siena, at Piazza Antonio Gramsci and Piazza San Domenico. Bus information kiosks are on site there.

Coaches Throughout Tuscany

Bus service operates more or less throughout Tuscany. Major bus companies include:

- **FLORENCE**

  SITA: Via Santa Caterina da Siena 15r, SMN, Florence, 800-373.760, *www.sitabus.it*

  LAZZI: Piazza della Stazione 3r, corner Piazza Adua, SMN, Florence, 055-215.155, *www.lazzi.it*

  CAP: Largo fratelli Alinari, 9, Florence, 055-214.637, *www.capautolinee.it*

- **SIENA**

  TRAIN: Piazza Antonio Gramsci, 0577-204.228, *www.trainspa.it*

- **PISA**

  CPT: Piazza Sant'Antonio 1, 800-012.773 or 050-884.111, *www.cpt.pisa.it*

  LAZZI: Piazza Sant'Antonio 1, 050-462.88, *www.lazzi.it*

- **GROSSETO**

  Rama: Via Topazo 12, Grosseto, 199-848.787, *www.ramamobilita.it*

Taxis

Cabs are expensive and hard to find in **Florence**. Official taxis are white with "Taxi" on the roof. In **Florence** there are taxi ranks in Piazza SMN, Piazza San Marco, Piazza della Stazione, Piazza del Duomo, Piazza della Repubblica, Piazza Santa Croce, and Piazza di Santa Trinità. In **Siena**, taxis line up at Piazza Matteotti and Piazza della Stazione; in **Pisa**, at Piazza del Duomo, Piazza Garibaldi, and Piazza della Stazione.

To call a cab: **Florence** Radiotaxi *(055-4390, 055-4798, 055-4242)*; **Siena** Radiotaxi *(0577-49222)*; **Pisa** Radiotaxi *(050-541.600 or 050-561.878)*. Beware: the meter starts running from the time you call.

Car/Bike/Moped Rentals

The best way to get around Tuscany is by car. Despite notions to the contrary, Italian drivers are excellent and courteous. Most car rental agencies in Florence are near the SMN train station. While driving is great in Tuscany, it can be a hassle in Florence. For Traffic-Free Zones (ZTL), parking, and other restrictions, check with the traffic police, or **Vigili Urbani** *(055-32831)*. For roadside assistance, contact the **Automobile Club d'Italia** *(ACI, Viale Amendola 36, Florence, 055-24861; 24-hour emergency: 803-116)*. ACI has reciprocal agreements with AAA and other auto clubs, entitling members to free basic repairs and lowered fees for other services.

- **Avis** *(www.avis.com)*: Borgo Ognissanti 128r, SMN, Florence, 055-213.629; Florence Airport, 055-315.588; Pisa Airport, 050-42028; Via Simone Martini 36, Siena, 0577-270.305

- **Europcar** *(www.europcar.com)*: Borgo Ognissanti 53-55r, SMN, Florence, 055-290.438; Florence Airport, 055-318.609; Pisa Airport, 050-41081

- **Hertz** *(www.hertz.com)*: Via Maso Finiguerra 33, SMN, Florence, 055-239.8205; Florence Airport, 055-307.370

- **Maggiore** *(www.maggiore.it)*: Via Maso Finiguerra 13r, Florence, 055-294.578

- **Maxirent Car & Scooter Rental** *(www.maxirent.com)*: Borgo Ognissanti 133r, SMN, Florence, 055-265.4207

- **Alinari Scooter Rental** *(www.alinarirental.com)*: Via San Zanobi 38r, Florence, 055-280.500

- **Florence by Bike** *(www.florencebybike.it)*: Via San Zanobi 120r, Florence, 055-488.992

- **DF Bike** *(www.dfbike.it)*: Strada Massetana Romana 54, Siena, 0577-271.905

- **Automotocicli Perozzi** *(www.perozzi.it)*: Via del Romitorio 5, Siena, 0577-280.839, or 0577-223.157

Gas Stations

Many gas stations close from noon to 3:30PM, then are open until about 7:30PM. Most are closed on Sundays. There is a 24-hour AGIP gas station in Florence at Viale dei Mille *(055-587.091)*. *Senza piombo* means "lead-free gas."

Florentine Street Numbers

Foreigners, beware! During 19th-century urban renewal in Florence, commercial street numbers were red and denoted by an "r" (for *rosso,* red) and residential numbers were black, noted by an "n" (for *nero*, black) or just the number. This system continues, creating confusion for foreigners when the numbers seem to follow no logical order.

MAKING PHONE CALLS

Local area codes begin with a 0 (e.g., 055 for Florence, 050 for Pisa). When dialing within Italy, even locally, include the area code. When calling direct from the U.S., dial 011-39 (Italy's country code), then the entire local number, including the 0. Italian 800 numbers are toll-free. For international calls from Italy, dial 00 plus country code (1 for U.S.), area code, and number.

Tuscan Dialing Codes:

Arezzo: 0575	Florence: 055
Lucca: 0583	Pisa: 050
Pistoia: 0573	Siena: 0577
Viareggio: 0584	

MEALS

In Italy pasta is a course, not a meal. The main courses are: *antipasto* (appetizer), *primo* (small pasta portion), and *secondo* (entrée). It's usual in Italy to eat a *primo* and *secondo*. And don't forget the *dolci* (desserts)!

SHOPPING

HOURS: Shops usually open at 9AM or 10AM and close at 7PM or 7:30PM, M–Sa. Most close for lunch at 1PM–3:30PM or 2PM–4PM. In summer they are closed on Saturday afternoons; the rest of the year, on Monday mornings. *Chiuso per Ferie* means the shop is closed for vacation, mostly August, sometimes July.

TAX REFUNDS: Non-EU citizens can get a refund for part of the sales tax when spending more than €150 at a store. Show your passport and ask for a tax refund form in the store. When leaving Italy, go to the Italian customs office (Global Refund Office) at the airport and have your form stamped. You'll have to show your passport and store receipt. You may have to show your purchases, so it's best to do this before check-in or else keep your purchases in your carry-on. Once home, return one copy of the form in the envelope provided and keep the other copy for yourself. If traveling to other EU countries, get your forms stamped in the airport customs office of the last EU country you leave. It takes about three months to get the refund.

SPECIALTIES: Artisanal crafts flourish throughout Tuscany. The region is famous for its superbly made leather goods; silks, woolens, and other textiles; stationery and paper goods; and decorative and practical objects made of wood, glass, and metals. Don't forget the fabled Tuscan cuisine and the splendid wines, grown in one of the world's most renowned wine producing areas.

DESIGNER OUTLETS: Designer outlets outside Florence offer good deals, often with extra discounts at the cash register. It's a hit-or-miss operation, but when you find the perfect Prada coat, Bottega Veneta bag, or Ferragamo shoes at 30% to 70% off, you'll go home happy. South of the city are **Space**, the Prada Outlet *(Località Levanella, Montevarchi, 055-978.781; call for hours, usually open daily)*, as well as Miu Miu, Jil Sander, and Helmut Lang outlets in Montevarchi, and **The Mall** *(Via Europa 8, Leccio, Reggello, 055-865.7775; call for hours, usually 10AM–7PM daily)*, in Leccio, which has outlets of many Italian and international designers. North of the city is the **Barberino Outlet** *(Via Meucci, Barberino del Mugello, 055-842.161, www.mcarthurglen.it/barberino; hours: Tu–F 10AM–8PM, Sa–Su 10AM–9PM; Dec–Jan, June–Sep, also M 2PM–8PM)*, with over 100 stores. Drive, take a train and taxi, or ask at major hotels or the Tourist Office for organized tours or private drivers. For best shopping locations in Italy, buy *Lo Scopri Occasioni*,

the shopper's bible, available in English in major Italian bookstores.

DEPARTMENT STORES: La Rinascente and Coin are Italy's largest chain department stores. Upim is a chain discount store.

COOKING CLASSES

Dying to learn some of the culinary secrets of Tuscan cuisine? Take a cooking class! Chef Silvia Maccari, a TV personality and cookbook author, takes you to the San Lorenzo farmer's market, teaches you Florentine recipes, and then you eat! She also offers a class in kosher Italian cooking. Chef Claudio Piantini, owner of Ristorante Torre Guelfa, outside Florence, guides you through some of the recipes that made him a rising culinary star. After a trip to the Sant'Ambrogio farmer's market, Chef Barbara Desderi invites you into her home to learn a few secrets of the Tuscan epicure. Cooking and wine-tasting classes are available in various parts of Tuscany through **The International Kitchen** *(800-945-8606 or 312-467-0560, www.theinternational kitchen.com)*, based in Chicago.

LODGINGS

Agriturismo is the system whereby farms offer meals made of ingredients produced on site; many also provide lodgings in converted farmhouses. Invariably, they are a wonderful way to visit the region's countryside, enjoy genuine local gastronomy and wine, and have, for a small moment, an insider's view of Tuscany. Internet prices are cheaper, so try booking through the tourist office's site, *www.toscanaeturismo.net*. In Florence, you can get help finding accommodations at the **Consorzio Informazioni Turistiche Alberghiere** *(ITA: 055-282.893)*, the tourist board's hotel help office, in the Santa Maria Novella train station, by Track 9.

SAY IT IN ITALIANO

A phrase book can be very helpful, but here's a short list of basic words and phrases.

Parla inglese? *(PAR-lah een-GLAY-zeh)* Do you speak English?

Buon giorno *(boo-ohn GEOR-no)* Good morning (before lunch)

Buona sera *(boo-ohna SEHR-ah)* Good afternoon/evening (after lunch)

Buona notte *(boo-ohna NOH-tay)* Good night

Arrivederci *(ah-ree-veh-DEHR-chee)* Good-bye

Ciao *(CHOW)* Hi!/Bye

Per favore *(pair fah-VOH-reh)* Please

Vorrei *(voh-RAY)* I'd like

Grazie *(GRAH-tsee-yay)* Thank you

Prego *(PREY-go)* You're welcome

Permesso *(pair-MESS-oh)* Excuse me (to move past someone in a crowd)

19

Mi scusi *(me SCOO-zee)* Excuse me (to get attention; sorry)

Mi dispiace *(me dees-pee-YA-cheh)* I'm sorry

Va bene *(vah BEH-neh)* OK, That's OK

Aspetta *(ahss-PET-ah)* Wait

Andiamo *(ahn-dee-YA-moh)* Let's go

Sì *(SEE)* Yes

No *(NOH)* No

Dov'è … *(doh-VEH)* Where is …

la metropolitana *(la metro-polee-TAH-na)* subway

metro *(met-ROH)* subway (short version)

un biglietto *(oon bee-LEEYE-toh)* a ticket

la strada *(la STRAH-da)* the street

via *(VEE-yah)* street (name)

l'albergo *(l'ahl-BEAR-goh)* hotel

il negozio *(il neh-GOH-tsee-oh)* store

il ristorante *(il ree-stoh-RAHN-teh)* restaurant

il palazzo *(il pah-LAH-tsoh)* apartment building; palace; mansion

la piazza *(la pee-AH-tsah)* square (town square)

Dove sono i gabinetti? *(DOH-veh SOH-noh ee gab-ee-NET-ee)* Where is the bathroom?

Quanto costa? *(KWAN-toh COST-ah)* How much does it cost?

Signora *(see-NYO-rah)* Ma'am, Mrs.

Signorina *(see-nyo-REE-nah)* Miss

Signor/Signore *(see-NYO-reh)* Mr., Sir

cameriere *(kahm-air-ee-AIR-eh)* waiter

cameriera *(kahm-ahr-ee-AIR-ah)* waitress

chi *(KEE)* who

cosa *(KOH-ZA)* what

Cos'è? *(koz-EH)* What is it?

dove *(DOH-veh)* where

come *(KOH-meh)* how

quanti *(KWAHN-tee)* many, how many

quanto *(KWAHN-toh)* much, how much

quando *(KWAHN-doh)* when

colazione *(koh-lah-tsee-OH-neh)* breakfast

pranzo *(PRAHN-tsoh)* lunch

cena *(CHEH-na)* dinner

ETIQUETTE TIPS

When entering or leaving a shop always say, "Buon giorno" (good morning—before lunch) or "Buona sera" (good afternoon—after lunch). Before handling merchandise, ask, "Posso?" (May I?). It's polite to use the appropriate form of address. Use "Signore" for men, "Signora" for women, or "Signorina" for young women.

To get the attention of a waiter, call out, "Senta!" (literally, "Listen!") or "Scusi!" ("Excuse me").

Dress code: Shorts, bare shoulders, or provocative clothing are not allowed in churches.

TOURIST INFORMATION

There are tourist information offices of the **Azienda Promozionale Turistica (APT)** *(www.firenzeturismo.it)* or **Ufficio Informazioni Turistiche** at the Florence and Pisa airports and at the following addresses in Florence:

- Via Cavour 1r, 055-290.832, *www.firenze.turismo.toscana.it*; hours: M–Sa 8:30AM–6:30PM, Sundays & holidays 8:30AM–1PM

- Borgo Santa Croce 29r, 055-234.0444; hours: summer M–Sa 9AM–7PM, Su 9AM–2PM; winter, M–Sa 9AM–5PM

- Piazza della Stazione 4, 055-212.245; hours: M–Sa 8:30AM–7PM, Su 8:30AM–2PM

- Via Portigiani 3, outside the City Gates, 055-597.8373; hours: M–Sa 9AM–1PM

Vigili Urbani vans with **APT** staff offer help and information for tourists. They operate from Easter through September, 8AM–7PM daily, in Piazza della Repubblica, on Via Calzaiuoli, and on Via Guicciardini just south of Ponte Vecchio.

Italian Tourist Offices in the USA:
New York: 212-245-5618/4822
Los Angeles: 310-820-1898/0098
Chicago: 312-644-0996/0990
Toronto: 416-925-4882/3870
www.italiantourism.com

TICKET AGENCIES
Tickets for concerts, plays, and exhibits can be bought at **Box Office Srl** (*Via Alamanni 39, Santa Maria Novella area, 055-210.804, www.boxol.it*).

SEASONAL EVENTS

May, September, and October are generally the best months to visit Florence, mostly because the summer is not only hot but also packed with tourists. *Firenze Spettacolo* (in kiosks or at *www.firenzespettacolo.it*, in Italian) lists music and other cultural events in the city. It also publishes *Info Florence*, a free guide. Throughout the year in Florence and Tuscany there are notable festivals and events. Check local listings, tourist office information, and *www.toscanamusiche.it* for concerts in churches, cloisters, and monasteries as well as street concerts. You can also check Musicus Concentus *(www.musicusconcentus.com)* for music events in Florence throughout the year. Be sure to consult posters and pick up guides at local tourist offices. If you're lucky, you might catch one of the many *sagre* (rites) celebrating local food specialties.

Spring:

Holy Week (week preceding Easter)—Religious processions, often in Renaissance costume, occur in towns throughout Tuscany, with stagings of scenes from the life of Christ on Good Friday in San Gimignano and Grassina. Larger celebrations occur in places like Bagno a Ripoli (outside Florence), Buonconvento (near Siena), and Castiglion Fiorentino (near Arezzo).

Explosion of the Cart: Scoppio del Carro (Easter Sunday)— This 12th-century rite begins with a parade, including musicians and flag throwers, through the city to bring a wooden cart pulled by oxen, the *carro*, from one end of Florence to Piazza del Duomo. At mass *(11AM)*, a priest sets a mechanical dove in motion, which flies to the *carro*, setting off fireworks *(Piazzale della Porta al Prato to Piazza del Duomo, Florence).*

Plant and Flower Show: Mostra Mercato di Piante e Fiori (late April/early May, early October)—This 1859 garden, with its fabulous glass house, hosts a spectacular plant and flower show. Growers from around Tuscany participate *(Giardino di Orticoltura, Via Vittorio Emanuele 4, outside city gates, Florence, 055-480.469, Bus 4).*

Musical May: Maggio Musicale Fiorentino (late April– late June)—This two-month festival of opera, music, and dance showcases international artists. Two free events (ballet and music) in Piazza della Signoria close the season *(Teatro del Maggio Musicale Fiorentino,*

Corso Italia 16, Florence, 055-277.9350, www.maggio fiorentino.com).

Palazzo Corsini Crafts Fair: Artigianato e Palazzo (mid-May weekend)—Artisans from around Italy sell their wares at this lovely crafts fair *(Palazzo Corsini, Via della Scala, Florence, 055-265.4588, www.artigianatoepalazzo.it).*

Mille Miglia (Saturday, late May)—A 1,000-mile race of vintage cars starts and ends in Brescia (northern Italy); a stunning array of fabulous old models makes its way through Florence from Porta Romana, across Santa Trinità bridge, to Piazza della Signoria *(Florence 010-576.1799, www.1000miglia.eu).*

Winery Open Houses: Cantine Aperte (last Sunday in May)—Open wine tastings take place on vinicultural estates. Get a guide at tourist offices *(throughout Tuscany, 075-988.9529, www.movimentoturismovino.it).*

Summer:

Dance and Theatre Festival: Fabbrica Europa (May–June)—Enjoy innovative theater and dance *(Stazione Leopolda, Teatro Affratellamento and other spaces, Florence, 055-248.0515, www.fabbricaeuropa.net, Bus 7)*.

Luminara di San Ranieri (June 16)—This festival is replete with candlelight and a boat race *(Pisa, along the river Arno 050-910.393/506, www.comune.pisa.it)*.

Jousting Matches: Giostra del Saracino (third Saturday in June, first Sunday in September)—The 13th-century sport starts at 5PM, with parades at 10AM and 2:30PM *(P.za Grande, Arezzo, 0575-377.462, www.giostradel saracino.arezzo.it)*.

Ceramics Festival: Festa Internazionale della Ceramica (mid–late June, 8 days)—Renaissance music and costumes enliven this ceramics fair in a town renowned for its production of ceramics *(Montelupo, 0571-518.993, www.comune.montelupo-fiorentino.fi.it)*.

Florence Dance Festival (July, December)—Performances feature contemporary, traditional, and classical dance by international stars, with arrangements by emerging choreographers. The setting is Fiesole's ancient Roman amphitheatre *(Teatro Romano, Via Portigiani 1, Fiesole, 055-289.276, www.florencedance.org)*.

Siena Horse Race: Palio, Siena (July 2, August 16)—The pageantry and processional last over four hours; the bareback horse race itself, less than two minutes. It's worth the fanfare to watch the flag throwers do their thing *(P.za del Campo, Siena, www.ilpalio.org)*.

Medieval Festival (mid-July)—Medieval life in Monteriggioni takes over, with period dress, music, dancing, food, and crafts *(Monteriggioni, 0577-304.834)*.

Pistoia Blues (mid-July, one weekend)—Local and international musicians entertain the crowds *(Pistoia, 0573-216.22, www.pistoiablues.com)*.

Joust of the Bear: Giostra dell'Orso (July 25)—A month of concerts, pageants, and fairs ends with this joust, in which 12 knights face a "bear" (made of wood) *(Pistoia, 0573-216.22)*.

Chamber Music Festival: Incontri in Terra di Siena (late July)—South of Siena, near Montepulciano and Arezzo, the estate of La Foce hosts this festival. A Renaissance villa, medieval castle, frescoed chapel, and English garden are among the highlights *(La Foce, Val d'Orcia, 0578-691.01, www.lafoce.com)*.

Concerts in the Abbeys: Estate Musicale Chigiana (July–August)—Hear classical music played in ethereal settings *(Siena, 0577-220.91, www.chigiana.it)*.

Puccini Opera Festival (July–August)—The open-air theater in the town where Puccini lived, not far from his native Lucca, stages the composer's operas and features internationally acclaimed singers *(Torre del Lago Puccini, 0584-359.322, www.puccinifestival.it)*.

Tuscan Sun Festival (first two weeks of August)—This is a festival of music, film, talks, food, and wine, co-directed by Frances Mayes, author of *Under the Tuscan Sun* *(Cortona, 0575-627.67, www.tuscansunfestival.com)*.

Autumn:

Musical September: Settembre Musica (September)— Enjoy early music concerts *(Teatro della Pergola & elsewhere, Florence, 055-608.420, www.amicimusica.fi.it)*.

World Music Festival: Rassegna Internazionale Musica dei Popoli (October–November)—Innovative international performers are featured *(Auditorium FLOG, Via M. Mercati 24B, outside the city gates, Florence, 055-487.145, www.flog.it)*.

Winter:

Florence Film Festival: Festival dei Popoli (November or December)—The city hosts an international drama and documentary film festival (some films are dubbed in Italian) *(various clubs and cinemas, Florence, 055-244.778, www.festivaldeipopoli.org)*.

Carnival in Viareggio: Carnevale di Viareggio (Four Sundays in February/early March)—These festive carnivals date back to 1873. Vibrant parades showcase extravagant, huge floats. Street parties, fireworks, masked balls, and cultural events add to the lively atmosphere *(Viareggio, Fondazione Carnevale Viareggio: 0584-184.0755, www.viareggio.ilcarnevale.com)*.

FLORENCE AND TUSCANY'S TOP PICKS

TOP PICK!

Florence and Tuscany offer an abundance of one-of-a-kind attractions and experiences for visitors. Here are some of the top picks not to be missed!

Florence:

★ **Duomo Santa Maria del Fiore** *(see page 39)*
★ **Baptistery of San Giovanni** *(see page 39)*
★ **Piazza della Signoria** *(see page 41)*
★ **Uffizi Gallery** *(see page 42)*
★ **Ponte Vecchio** *(see page 43)*
★ **Bargello Museum** *(see page 44)*
★ **Santa Maria Novella** *(see page 51)*
★ **Santa Croce** *(see page 63)*
★ **Basilica San Lorenzo & Medici Chapels** *(see page 76)*
★ **San Marco** *(see page 79)*
★ **Galleria dell'Accademia** *(see page 79)*
★ **Brancacci Chapel** *(see page 93)*
★ **Palazzo Pitti** *(see page 94)*

Tuscany:

> You may have the universe
> if I may have Italy.
>
> *–Giuseppe Verdi*

Part I: Florence

Cradle of the Renaissance, Florence is perhaps one of the world's greatest tributes to the creativity of the human spirit. The brilliance of some of the West's finest minds and the genius of its artists are nowhere so evident. Dante, Giotto, Boccaccio, Brunelleschi, Ghiberti, Fra Angelico, Masaccio, Leon Battista Alberti, Botticelli, da Vinci, Savonarola, Macchiavelli, Michelangelo, Galileo, Verdi, and Puccini are only some of the many notables who made Florence the Athens of the modern age.

In 59 B.C., Julius Caesar founded Florentia on the site of an ancient settlement. By the 14th century, Florence was the strongest financial center of Europe. Its currency, the gold florin, was used internationally. And thanks to Dante, Florentine Italian was used throughout Italy. But it wasn't until the patronage of the Medicis that intellectual acumen, artistic genius, political power, and financial capital coalesced, and the Renaissance was born on the banks of the Arno in the flourishing town known as Firenze. The legacy of that genius is part of what makes this city so magical. Cocooned amid verdant hills, suffused in an ethereal amber light, remarkable Florence is possessed of a spirit forged in the grand tradition of Humanism.

With greatness, however, comes rivalry, and Florence had its fair share. The Guelfs (papists) *vs.* the Ghibellines (pro-Holy Roman Emperor), Florence *vs.* Siena *vs.* Pisa *vs.* Lucca, Brunelleschi *vs.* Ghiberti, Lorenzo the Magnificent's splendor *vs.* Savonarola the Avenger's puritanism—feuds and competition fueled both the grandiose and the grotesque here. Unsurprisingly, the word *snob* was coined in Florence: an abbreviation for the merchant class, the *nouveau riche* who were not of noble birth, *s.nob* stood for "*senza nobiltà.*"

Today, while the titans of the Renaissance are long gone, the sensibilities they bequeathed to humanity are expressed through a tradition of artisanal crafts, or *artigianato.* Handmade creations of leather, silk, fabric, wood, paper, glass, and other materials are exquisitely fashioned in workshops, or *bottegas,* around the city and throughout Tuscany. Whether in past grandeur or present endeavor, in great masterpieces or small creations, art and aesthetics thrive in Florence. It is a city that shows us how to appreciate the genius and beauty of everyday living.

chapter 1

CENTRO STORICO
SANTA MARIA NOVELLA
SANTA CROCE

CENTRO STORICO SANTA MARIA NOVELLA SANTA CROCE

Places to See:

1. DUOMO SANTA MARIA DEL FIORE ★
2. BAPTISTERY OF SAN GIOVANNI ★
3. Museo dell'Opera del Duomo
4. Badia Fiorentina
5. Orsanmichele
6. PIAZZA DELLA SIGNORIA ★
7. Palazzo Vecchio
8. UFFIZI GALLERY ★
9. Vasari Corridor
10. PONTE VECCHIO ★
11. Palazzo Nonfinito
12. BARGELLO MUSEUM ★
13. Dante House
14. Museo di Storia della Scienza (Galileo Museum)
15. Santo Stefano al Ponte
49. SANTA MARIA NOVELLA ★
50. Ognissanti
51. Museo Marino Marini
52. Palazzo Rucellai
53. Palazzo Corsini
54. Santa Trinità
55. Museo Ferragamo

56. Palazzo Davanzati
57. Piazza della Repubblica
58. Teatro Comunale
59. Alinari National Museum of Photography (MNAF)
60. Palazzo Strozzi
61. Cinema Odeon
117. SANTA CROCE ★
118. Casa Buonarroti
119. San Remigio
120. Museo Horne
121. Museo di Firenze Com'Era
122. Teatro Verdi

Places to Eat & Drink:

16. Cocquinarius
17. Le Mossacce
18. Paoli
19. Il Pennello
20. Frescobaldi Ristorante & Wine Bar
21. Cantinetta dei Verrazzano
22. Perchè No!
23. Gelateria Caffè delle Carrozze
24. Caruso Jazz Café
25. Astor Caffè
26. Angels

★ *Top Picks*

Where to Shop:

Where to Stay:

CENTRO STORICO

Bus: 1, 6, 14, 17, 23, A, B

• SNAPSHOT •

The living history of Italian art and architecture is on display everywhere in Florence. The historical center, dominated by the superb Duomo, is densely packed with imposing palaces and stunning examples of architectural beauty. While some historic buildings are closed to the public, their external elegance is available for all to appreciate. The most important and distinctive landmarks are noted in the following pages, but Florence generously offers a masterpiece at literally every step. Its legacy of brilliance, passion, and invention remains with us in the creations of genius that line its streets and buildings. In the city's historical center, that legacy constantly touches our core, reminding us of the palpable and intangible ways art brings us closer to our humanity. Walk leisurely through this open-air panorama of history, art, and beauty, and take your time in absorbing the experience.

PLACES TO SEE
Landmarks:

From just about any street in the historic center of Florence you can glimpse the ★**DUOMO SANTA MARIA DEL FIORE (1)** *(Piazza del Duomo, 055-230.2885, www.operaduomo.firenze.it; hours: M–W, F, 10AM–5PM, Th 10AM–3:30PM, July–Sep 10AM–5PM, other months 10AM–4:30PM, Sa 10AM–4:45PM, May & Oct, Su 1:30–4:45PM).* Enormous, with intricate patterns and wonderful carvings in white, green, and red marble, it is topped by Brunelleschi's famous **Cupola**, or **Dome** *(hours: M–F 8:30AM–7PM, Sa 8:30AM–5:40PM),* the stunning octagonal masterpiece that dominates the Florentine skyline. Too large to build with supports or scaffolding, the dome is a remarkable engineering achievement. If you can manage the 463 steps, it's a marvelous spot from which to behold the city and its environs. Equally famous is the cathedral's bell tower, the **Campanile** *(hours: M–Su 8:30AM–7:30PM),* one of Italy's most beautiful, designed by Giotto with fabulous standing sculptures and bas-reliefs. Brave its 414 steep, narrow steps, and you'll be rewarded with another stunning view.

Facing the Duomo's main entrance is the ★**BAPTISTERY OF SAN GIOVANNI (2)** *(hours: M–Sa 12:15–7PM, Su 8:30AM–2PM, first Sa of month 8:30AM–2PM),* an octagon famous for its gilded bronze doors. The Gothic south (entrance) doors were done by Andrea Pisano nearly

TOP PICK!

TOP PICK!

100 years before Lorenzo Ghiberti created the north doors. Ghiberti's east doors, dubbed the "**Gates of Paradise**" by Michelangelo, are artistic masterpieces embodying the then-emerging concepts of Renaissance aesthetics. When young Ghiberti won the competition for the doors, Brunelleschi was distressed—until he was given the task of creating the overpowering Dome. The Baptistery's east doors are copies of the original **Gates of Paradise**, which are located in the **Museo dell'Opera del Duomo (3)** *(Piazza del Duomo 9, 055-230.2885, www.operaduomo. firenze.it; hours: M–Sa 9AM–7:30PM, Su 9AM–1:45PM).* Besides Ghiberti's gates, don't miss Donatello's shockingly realistic wooden Mary Magdalen and the various Michelangelo pieces. Of the latter, the *Pietà Bandini*, with Christ slipping from the grasp of Nicodemus, was to have been Michelangelo's tombstone. Nicodemus, in fact, is a likeness of the sculptor so obsessed with his work that he smashed Christ's left arm in frustration. His servant is said to have retrieved the pieces and restored the arm.

Badia Fiorentina (4) *(Via Dante Alighieri, 055-264.402; hours: Su–M 3PM–6PM, Tu–Sa 6:30AM–6PM; cloister: M 3PM–6PM),* a medieval Benedictine abbey and the city's oldest monastery, was founded by Willa, a noblewoman convinced by a monk who decried the clergy's evil ways and urged aristocrats to build monasteries. Her son, Ugo, was considered a visionary; as a child he was able to identify the father he never saw when the man returned from exile demanding this "paternity test"; little Ugo, of course, had some help from Mom. The abbey houses lovely frescoes in the cloister, a painting by Filippino Lippi, and a lovely marble relief by Mino da Fiesole.

A 14th-century grain market, the church of **Orsanmichele (5)** *(Via dell'Arte della Lana 1, 055-284.944; hours: church Tu–Su 10AM–5PM, museum M 10AM–5PM)* was closely linked to the guilds, which commissioned statues of their patron saints. Art was a means for politicos—Guelfs, Ghibellines, Medicis, popes, you name it—to exert influence. The museum contains Botticelli frescoes, copies of Donatello statues and reliefs (including his *St. George*, the first relief to employ perspective; it's also an early Renaissance masterpiece of psychological realism), and Ghiberti's bronze *St. John the Baptist*.

★**PIAZZA DELLA SIGNORIA (6)** is a veritable open-air sculpture gallery. Some originals, some copies, the statues tell the story of Florence's glorious past. Michelangelo's *David* in the piazza is a copy; the original statue is in the Accademia *(see page 79)*. Works by Donatello, Giambologna, Cellini, Ammannati, and Orcagna, among others, are also on display. Cellini nearly destroyed his house while making his famous bronze *Perseus*: to cast the triumphant warrior holding up the head of Medusa

TOP PICK!

after slaying the gorgon, Cellini had to stoke his furnace to such intensity that it burned his roof. From the 14th century to modern times, Florentine civic life centered around **Piazza della Signoria (6)**, where citizens gathered when called to a *parlamento*, or public meeting. The piazza formed when Guelfs demolished Ghibelline homes in the area in 1268, creating a lopsided "square." More than two centuries later, religious reformer Girolamo Savonarola lit his "Bonfire of the Vanities," protesting wickedness and wastefulness, especially of the clergy and the wealthy classes. That didn't go over well: the next year, in 1498, he was hung and burned at the stake in the same spot on the piazza. The Signoria, the city's supreme governing body, sat in the **Palazzo Vecchio (7)** *(Piazza Signoria, 055-276.8325; hours: M–W, F–Sa 9AM–7PM, Th, Su 9AM–2PM)*, now city hall. The **Salone dei Cinquecento** (Hall of the Five Hundred), where the Great Council once met, is covered in Vasari frescoes. Upstairs in the **Sala dei Gigli** (Room of the Lilies), Ghirlandaio frescoes alternate with gold fleurs-de-lis, an emblem of Florence.

In the late 1500s, Duke Cosimo I de' Medici had Vasari build offices *(uffici)* at the southern end of **Piazza della Signoria (6)**, the glass-walled upper floor of which was a gallery for the Medicis' art collection. Now the world's foremost museum of Renaissance art, the ★**UFFIZI GALLERY (8)** *(Piazzale degli Uffizi 6, 055-294.883, www.uffizi.com, www.polomuseale. firenze.it; hours: Tu–Su 8:15AM–6:50PM, call ahead or go online for reservations to avoid long*

TOP PICK!

lines) contains masterpieces by Masolino, Masaccio, Veneziano, Uccello, Lippi, Botticelli, da Vinci, Michelangelo, and Bellini, among other Renaissance artists, as well as works from other periods by Giotto, Cimabue, Martini, da Fabriano, Titian, del Sarto, Parmigianino, Rubens, van Dyck, Velázquez, Gentileschi, Caravaggio, and many others. Among the highlights: Lippi's *Madonna and Child with Angels*; Botticelli's *The Birth of Venus*, *Primavera*, and *Adoration of the Magi*; Michelangelo's *The Holy Family*; Raphael's *Madonna of the Goldfinch*; and Titian's *The Venus of Urbino*.

To avoid the stench of the river's tanneries during his trek from work in **Palazzo Vecchio (7)** to home in the **Palazzo Pitti** *(see page 94)*, Cosimo I had Vasari build an elevated passageway in 1565. The **Vasari Corridor (9)** *(Firenze Musei: 055-294.883; call for tours or check Web site: www.polomuseale.firenze.it)* is open for guided tours only and now houses a collection of paintings. The corridor links the **Uffizi (8)** to **Palazzo Pitti**, crossing the Arno atop Florence's oldest bridge, the ★**PONTE VECCHIO (10)**. The bridge's 16th-century tanners, butchers, and blacksmiths have long since been replaced by jewelers. Like a small city spanning the

TOP PICK!

water, the famous medieval bridge with its overhanging buttressed workshops and soaring arches offers great views of the river and is alive with painters, street vendors, and tourists. It was Florence's only Arno bridge left intact during World War II.

Arts & Entertainment:

Palazzo Nonfinito (11) or "Unfinished Palace" *(Via del Proconsolo 12, 055-239.6449; hours: Su–T, Th–F 9AM–1PM, Sa 9AM–5PM)*, Italy's first anthropological museum, features, among other things, art from former Italian colonies in Africa. Once city hall (in 1255), then a prison (16th century) and HQ of the *bargello*, or chief of police, the ★**BARGELLO MUSEUM (12)** *(Via del Proconsolo 4, 055-294.883, www.uffizi.com, www.polomuseale.firenze.it; hours: 8:15AM–2PM)* became a museum of Renaissance sculpture in 1865. This Gothic fortress is among the most important museums in Italy. Its unusual collection includes Michelangelo's first significant work, *Bacchus*, Donatello's two famous *Davids*, Verrocchio's *Lady with a Posy*, Giambologna's *Mercury*, works by Brunelleschi and the della Robbias, among many other masterpieces. Don't miss the Ivory Room, with its marvelous pieces from the Carrand collection. The two bronze panels, *The Sacrifice of Isaac*, were Brunelleschi's and Ghiberti's submissions for the competition to sculpt the Duomo Baptistery's north doors.

Dante House (13) *(Via S. Margherita 1, corner of Via Dante Alighieri, 055-219.416; call for hours)* is a museum dedicated to the poet's life, his years in exile, and Florentine

TOP PICK!

politics of his era. At **Palazzo Vecchio (7)** *(see page 42)*, the playrooms and puppet theatre in the children's museum **Museo dei Ragazzi** *(Palazzo Vecchio, Piazza della Signoria, 055-276.8224, www.museoragazzi.it; hours: 9AM–6PM)* are Renaissance-themed; workshops, talks, and historically geared multimedia games appeal to adults, too. Science and art overlap at the fascinating **Galileo Museum**, or **Museo di Storia della Scienza (14)** (History of Science Museum) *(Piazza dei Giudici 1, 055-265.311, www.museogalileo.it; hours: W–M 9:30AM–6PM, Tu 9:30AM–1PM)*, which features Galileo's instruments and models of his various experiments. Outstanding orchestral concerts are held at the ancient church of **Santo Stefano al Ponte (15)** *(Piazza Santo Stefano al Ponte, 055-290.832; call for information)*. If you tire of museums, do the Florentine thing: take an evening *passeggiata* (a gentle stroll) along **Via dei Calzaiuoli (30)** *(see also page 48)*.

PLACES TO EAT & DRINK
Where to Eat:

At the café/wine bar **Coquinarius (16)** (€€) *(Via delle Oche 15r, 055-230.2153; hours: M–Th 9AM–11PM, F–Sa 9AM–11:30PM, food served from 12PM, closed Aug)* the pastas are outstanding (try the pear and pecorino ravioli); good food and good wine mesh in a cozy atmosphere of bare brick walls and low-key jazz. **Le Mossacce (17)** (€) *(Via del Proconsolo 55r, 055-294.361, www.trattorialemossacce.it; hours: M–F lunch & dinner, closed Aug)* has excellent, authentic Florentine cuisine—from *ribollita*, the specialty black cabbage, bean, and vegetable soup, to *bistecca alla fiorentina* and *involtini*, beef wraps with artichoke stuffing. At **Paoli (18)** (€€) *(Via dei Tavolini 12r, 055-216.215; hours: W–M 12PM–2:30PM, 7PM–10:30PM, closed 3 wks in Aug)* the centuries-old palazzo with vaulted ceilings and frescoes is stupendous, but it's touristy and formal; try the spinach ravioli, mushroom risotto, or *entrecôte di manzo arlecchino* (thick steak with cognaccream sauce).

Don't miss the antipasti at **Il Pennello (19)** (€€) *(Via Dante Alighieri 4r, 055-294.848; hours: Tu–Sa 12PM–3PM, 7PM–10:30PM, closed Aug)*, Florence's oldest trattoria. **Frescobaldi Ristorante & Wine Bar (20)** (€€) *(Via dei Magazzini 2-4r, 055-284.724, www.frescobaldiwinebar.it; hours: M 7PM–12AM, Tu–Sa 12PM–12AM, closed 3 wks Aug)*, owned by a top Italian wine estate, offers their *vino* with cheeses, patés, and *salame*. Innovative dishes, like pumpkin ravioli in amaretto sauce, mix with more typical *tagliata di manzo* (thin steaks). Wood-paneled, chic, and popular, **Cantinetta dei Verrazzano (21)** (€) *(Via dei Tavolini 18r, 055-268.590, www.verrazzano.com; hours: 8AM–9PM)*, from another large wine producer, serves *focaccia* and *crostini* with great wines; there's also a bakery. Get your *gelato* two steps away at **Perchè No! (22)** (€) *(Via dei Tavolini 19r, 055-239.8969, www.percheno.firenze.it; hours: Su–M, W–F 12PM–10:30PM, Sa 12PM–11:30PM)*, an ice cream cognoscente's dream; try the *miele e sesamo semifreddo*, honey and sesame soft ice cream, or pistachio *gelato*. **Gelateria Caffè delle Carrozze (23) (€)** *(Piazza del Pesce 3-5r, 055-239.6810)* specializes in exotic fruit sorbets, and ice cream. Artist-owned **Caruso Jazz Café (24) (€-€€)** *(Via Lambertesca 15/16r, 055-267.0207, www.carusojazzcafe.com; hours: M–Sa 9:30AM–3:30PM, 6PM–11PM)*, with brick vaulted ceilings and big papier-mâché sculptures of city landmarks, is a hoot; it has light lunches, tea, jazz evenings, and Internet access.

Bars & Nightlife:

At the trendy jazz bar **Astor Caffè (25)** *(Piazza del Duomo 20r, 055-239.9000; hours: M–Sa 10AM–3AM, Su 5PM–3AM)*, chrome, glass, and a large skylight dominate; Internet access is a bonus. White canopies, white chairs, stone columns, and dramatic lighting set a stylish tone at **Angels (26)** *(Via del Proconsolo 29-31r, 055-239.8762, www.ristoranteangels.it; hours: 12PM–11:30PM)*; their restaurant serves Mediterranean food. Florence's first gay club, **Tabasco Disco Gay (27)** *(Piazza Santa Cecilia 3r, 055-213.000, www.tabascogay.it; hours: Tu–Su 10PM–6AM)* remains a popular gay/lesbian hangout, with techno and '70s disco music.

Florence's most famous café, **Café Rivoire (28)** *(Piazza della Signoria 5r, 055-214.412, www.rivoire.it; hours: Tu–Su 8AM–12AM)*, boasts the most expensive coffee in the city and a clientele of the rich, the famous, and the rest of us—all under the watchful eyes of Cellini's *Perseus* and the statues in the **Loggia dei Lanzi**. Check out the Art Deco chandelier at **Bar Perseo (29)** *(Piazza della Signoria 16r, 055-239.8316; hours: M–Sa 7AM–12AM)*, then have an *aperitivo*, homemade *gelato*, or sit outside and people-watch.

WHERE TO SHOP

Via dei Calzaiuoli (30) is lined with shops like Benetton, Diesel, Sisley, and Stefanel. Other good shopping streets in the area are **Via del Corso (31)**, **Via Calimala (32)**, and **Via Condotta (33)**. The chain **Il Papiro (34)** *(Piazza del Duomo 24r, 055-281.628, www.ilpapirofirenze.it)* carries typically Florentine marbled paper products. **Coin (35)** *(Via dei Calzaiuoli 56r, 055-280.531, www.coin.it; hours: M–Sa 10AM–7:30PM, Su 10:30AM–7:30PM)* is a popular department store. **Paperback Exchange (36)** *(Via*

delle Oche 4r, 055-293.460, www.papex. it; hours: M–F 9AM–7:30PM, Sa 10:30AM–7:30PM), the place for books in English, hosts readings and other events. It won't make you a Brunelleschi or da Vinci, but **Zecchi (37)** *(Via dello Studio 19r, 055-211.470, www.zecchi.it; hours: M–F 8:30AM–12:30PM, 3:30PM–7:30PM, Sa 8:30AM–12:30PM, closed Sa in Jul, closed Aug)* is famous for its art supplies. For three generations **Taddei (38)** *(Via Santa Margherita 11, 055-239.8960; hours: M–Sa 8AM–8PM, closed Aug)* has been creating marvelous handmade leather purses and boxes. **Bizzarri (39)** *(Via della Condotta 32r, 055-211.580, www. bizzarri-fi.biz; hours: M–F 9:30AM–1PM, 4PM–7:30PM,*

Sa 9:30AM–1PM, closed Aug) has every herbal product imaginable.

Tharros Bijoux (40) *(Vicolo de' Cerchi 2r, 055-284.126, www.tharros.com; hours: M–Sa 10AM–1PM, 3:30PM–7:30PM)* sells fabulous jewelry and museum reproductions. **Raspini Vintage (41)** *(Via Calimaruzza 17r, 055-213.901, www.raspini.com; hours: Tu–Sa 10:30AM–7:30PM, Su 2:30PM–7:30PM)* slashes prices on previous seasons' top Italian designer clothes and stock from **Raspini** stores *(Via Roma 25-29r, 055-213.077, www.raspini.com; hours: Su–M 2PM–7PM, Tu–Sa 10:30AM–7:30PM; Via Por Santa Maria 72r, 055-215.796; hours: Su–M 2:30PM–7:30PM, Tu–Sa 10:30AM–7:30PM; Via Martelli 5r, 055-239.8336; hours: M 3:30PM–7:30PM, Tu–Sa 9:30AM–1PM, 3:30PM–7:30PM, last Su of month 2PM–7PM)*. **Al Portico (42)** *(Piazza San Firenze 1, 055-213.716, www.semial portico.it; hours: M–F 8:30AM–7:30PM, Su 10AM–5PM)* enhances gardens with flowers, decorations, and ceramic pots. **Ponte Vecchio (10)** is the mecca of modern and antique jewelry—but beware: it's full of tourist traps.

WHERE TO STAY

In an historic 16th-century building, the elegant Palazzo Niccolini al Duomo (43) (€€€–€€€€) *(Via dei Servi 2, 055-282.412, www.niccolinidomepalace.com)*, replete with antiques, chandeliers, and period paintings, lives up to its aristocratic heritage. Cimatori Guest House (44) (€) *(Via Dante Alighieri 14, 055-265.5000, www.cimatori.it)*, a bare-bones bargain, is a walk-up (two to four floors). Cheery B&B **Dei Mori (45)** (€) *(Via Dante Alighieri 12, 055-211.438, www.deimori.com)*, located in a 19th-century building, is friendly and comfortable. **Hotel Aldini (46)** (€-€€) *(Via dei Calzaiuoli 13, 055-214.752, www.hotelaldini.it)* combines country furniture beautifully with terra-cotta floors. **Inpiazzadellasignoria (47)** (€€€) *(Via dei Magazzini 2, 055-239.9546, www.inpiazzadellasignoria.com)*, an elegant B&B (frescoes, antiques, marble bathrooms) is like a home of distinction. Simple, informal **Relais Uffizi (48)** (€€-€€€) *(Chiasso de' Baroncelli/Chiasso del Buco 16, 055-267.6239, www.relaisuffizi.it)* has well-appointed rooms on a quiet, charming street; the breakfast room looks onto fabulous Piazza della Signoria.

SANTA MARIA NOVELLA

Bus: 6, 11, 22, 36, 37, A, B, D

• SNAPSHOT •

The Santa Maria Novella quarter is Florence's poshest neighborhood, though the area around the train station, Santa Maria Novella, can be dodgy at night. Piazza di Santa Maria Novella has seen the rise of chic hotels and nightspots. Mansions and high-class hotels line the riverfront, typical of the opulence of this luxury district. Via Tornabuoni, home to designer showrooms, shines with *lusso* (luxury). Piazza Carlo Goldoni, the triangle formed by Via della Vigna Nuova, Via della Spada, and Via dei Fossi exudes elegance; it's a very upscale area, trendy both day and night, with designer boutiques, antique shops, cafés, and restaurants for the cognoscenti.

PLACES TO SEE
Landmarks:

A marvel of Gothic architecture, ★**SANTA MARIA NOVELLA (49)** *(Piazza di Santa Maria Novella, church: 055-215.918, www.smn.it; hours: M–Th, Sa 9AM–5PM, F, Su 1PM–5PM; museum:*

TOP PICK!

055-282.187; hours: M–Th, Sa 9AM–2PM, Su 8AM–1PM) is rich with several cloisters and chapels to explore. It contains numerous important artworks, including Ghirlandaio's *The Life of John the Baptist* fresco cycle and *The Life of the Virgin*, Masaccio's *Trinity*, and works by Filippino Lippi, Uccello, Nardo di Cione, and Andrea Orcagna. The opening of Boccaccio's *The Decameron* is set in the Filippo Strozzi Chapel. In Amerigo Vespucci's parish "Church of All Saints," **Ognissanti (50)** *(Borgo Ognissanti 42, 055-239.8700; hours: 8AM–12PM, 4PM–6:30PM; Cenacolo del Ghirlandaio, 055-294.883; hours: M–Tu, Sa 9AM–12PM)*, a Ghirlandaio fresco includes a portrait of this young navigator (in pink) as a boy. The boy went on to sail in Columbus's wake, and the American continents were named after him. Sandro Botticelli was buried here; his *St. Augustine* fresco is on the south wall. Ghirlandaio's *Last Supper* fresco is in the cloister next door.

Once the church of San Pancrazio, **Museo Marino Marini (51)** *(Piazza San Pancrazio, 055-219.432, www.museo marinomarini.it; hours: M, W–Sa 10AM–5PM)* displays this abstract artist's oeuvre. It includes his horse-and-rider bronzes, other bronze and cement sculptures, and paintings of dancers and jugglers. **Palazzo Rucellai (52)** *(Via della Vigna Nuova 18, closed to public)* was designed by architect Leon Battista Alberti in 1446 in Classical Roman style and features the Rucellai family emblem,

"Fortune's Sail," on its façade. One of the most majestic riverside mansions, **Palazzo Corsini (53)** *(Lungarno Corsini 10, entrance: Via del Parione 11, by appt only: 055-212.880, www.palazzocorsini.it)* houses the Corsini family's private art collection. Sumptuously Baroque, the palace was never a residence but served as an art gallery and a place for social entertaining. **Santa Trinità (54)** *(Piazza di Santa Trinità, 055-216.912; hours: M–Sa 8AM–12PM, 4PM–6PM, Su 4PM–6PM)*, with its ornate Baroque façade, is surprisingly simple inside, conducive to meditation.

More glamorous, the **Museo Ferragamo (55)** *(Piazza Santa Trinita 5r, entrance: Palazzo Spini Feroni, 055-336.0456, www.museoferragamo.it; hours: Sep–Jul W–M 10AM–6PM, Aug M–Sa 10AM–1PM, 2PM–6PM)*, located in the Palazzo Spini Feroni above the Ferragamo shoe shop, exhibits some of the most fabulous shoes in its 10,000-piece collection. It includes handmade shoes worn by Ingrid Bergman, Ava Gardner, and Rita Hayworth. Still partially under renovation, **Palazzo Davanzati (56)** *(Via Porta Rossa 13, 055-238.8610, www.polomuseale.firenze.it; hours: 8AM–1:50PM, closed 2nd, 4th Su and 1st, 3rd, 5th M of month)* takes you back in time to a wealthy 14th-century Florentine home. Part Medieval tower house, part Renaissance palace, its features include holes in the vaulted entranceway ceiling to throw objects at unwanted visitors. Frescoes, tapestries, paintings, and Renaissance furniture are displayed. In ancient times, the Roman forum was at **Piazza della Repubblica (57)**. The narrow streets and Jewish ghetto were razed at the close of the 19th century, and a grandiose arch and ostentatious square were built for the then-capital of Italy. Its many cafés, once attracting the intelligentsia, are still popular.

Arts & Entertainment:

May through June, one of Europe's oldest music festivals, **Maggio Musicale Fiorentino**, rivaling Salzburg and Bayreuth, takes place at **Teatro Comunale (58)** *(Corso Italia 16, 055-277.9350, www.maggiofiorentino.com; hours: Tu–F 10AM–4:30PM, Sa 10AM–1PM)*. Opera and ballet in the fall and symphony in the winter add to its renown. The world's oldest photography archive, **Alinari National Museum of Photography (MNAF) (59)** *(Piazza Santa Maria Novella 14Ar, 055-216.310, www.alinari fondazione.it; hours: Th–Tu 10AM–7PM)* owns nearly 3 million negatives and 900,000 vintage prints. Massive **Palazzo Strozzi (60)** *(Piazza degli Strozzi, 055-264.5155, www.palazzostrozzi.org; call for exhibit hours)*, perfectly Renaissance in style, stages art exhibits and fashion shows. **Cinema Odeon (61)** *(Via degli Anselmi, 055-214.068; call for showtimes)*, in Art Nouveau décor, runs original-language films.

PLACES TO EAT & DRINK
Where to Eat:

Trattoria Belle Donne (62) (€) *(Via delle Belle Donne 16r, 055-238.2609; hours: 12PM–2:30PM, 7PM–10:30PM, closed Aug)* is a great lunch option, with creative Tuscan dishes served at communal tables. A glamorous cellar with vaulted ceilings, **Buca Lapi (63) (€€€)** *(Via del Trebbio 1r, 055-213.768, www.bucalapi.com; hours: M–Sa 7PM–10:30PM)* has great food (try wild boar, *filetto di cinghiale* or stuffed rabbit, *coniglio ripieno*). **Cantinetta Antinori (64) (€€€)** *(Piazza Antinori 3, 055-292.234, www.antinori.it; hours: M–F 12PM–2:30PM, 7PM–10:30PM, closed 3 wks Aug & week of Christmas)*, another Florentine classic, uses ingredients from the Antinori farms and vineyards. **The Lounge (65) (€€€)** *(JK Place, Piazza Santa Maria Novella 9-10r, 055-264.5282, www.thelounge.it; hours: 12:30PM–12AM, closed 2 wks Aug)* has designer looks, a cool deck, and food using the best ingredients from around Italy. A gregarious owner, cozy cluttered rooms, and delicious food make **Trattoria Garga (66) (€€€)** *(Via del Moro 48r, 055-239.8898, www.garga.it; hours: 7PM 'til late)* a classic; try the *taglierini del Magnifico*, pasta in creamy orange and parmesan sauce.

Don't leave Florence without tasting the amazing *panini tartufati*, truffle sandwiches, with a glass of prosecco at **Procacci (67) (€)** *(Via de' Tornabuoni 64r, 055-211.656; hours: M–Sa 10:30AM–8PM, closed Aug)*. Roast meats and *melanzane alla parmigiana* are great at

Rosticceria della Spada (68) (€–€€) *(Via della Spada 62r, 055-218.757, www.laspadaitalia.com; hours: 12PM–3PM, 6PM–10:30PM)*; they do takeout at half-price. **Giacosa Roberto Cavalli (69) (€)** *(Via della Spada 10r, 055-277.6328, www.caffegiacosa.it; hours: summer M–Sa 7:30AM–12AM, winter M–Sa 7:30AM–8:30PM, closed 2 wks Aug)*, the Florentine designer's café, serves up fashion shows on a huge screen along with *bruschetta*. Famously popular, **Il Latini (70) (€€)** *(Via dei Palchetti 6r, 055-210.916, www.illatini.com; hours: Tu–Su 12:30PM–2:30PM, 7:30PM–10:30PM)* is exuberantly fun; try the *bistecca alla fiorentina*. In a 14th-century tower, **Al Lume di Candela (71) (€€€)** *(Via delle Terme 23r, 055-294.566; hours: M 7:30PM–11PM, Tu–Sa 12:30PM–2:30PM, 7:30PM–11PM, closed 2 wks Aug)* serves Tuscan and international dishes. Inventive twists on Tuscan classics add spice to the old-world elegance of **Oliviero (72) (€€€)** *(Via delle Terme 51r, 055-212.421, www.ristorante-oliviero.it; hours: M–Sa dinner, closed Aug)*, once preferred by Sophia Loren and Maria Callas.

The famous **Caffè Gilli (73) (€)** *(Piazza della Repubblica 39r/Via Roma 1r, 055-213.896, www.gilli.it; hours: W–M 8AM–12AM)*, in Belle Époque style, is great for coffee, pastries, and people-watching. **Giubbe Rosse (74) (€)** *(Piazza della Repubblica 13-14r, 055-212.280, www.giubberosse.it; hours: 7:30AM–2AM)* was the watering hole of writers, artists, and avant-garde futurists in the early 20th century. Lenin, Gorky, and other Russian revolutionaries allegedly gathered here. A national monument, **Caffè Concerto Paszkowski (75) (€)** *(Piazza della Repubblica 6r, 055-210.236, www. paszkowski.it; hours: Tu–Su 7AM–1AM)* has a live orchestra. Delicious Egyptian food, super-cheap, at **Amon (76) (€)** *(Via Palazzuolo 28r, 055-293.146; hours: Tu–Su 12PM–3PM, 6PM–11PM)* includes kebabs and falafel. **Pizzeria Funiculì (77) (€)** *(Via Il Prato 81r, 055-264.6553, www.pizzeriafuniculi.it; hours: M–F 12PM–3PM, 7PM–1AM, Sa–Su 7PM–1AM)*, huge and lively, is so good it's always packed.

Bars & Nightlife:

Straight from the Beat generation, brick cellar and all, **Art Bar (78)** *(Via del Moro 4r, 055-287.661; hours: M–Th 7PM–1AM, F–Sa 7PM–2AM, closed 3 wks Aug)* is a popular student hangout; the paintings on the walls were payment for drinks from 1950s artists who were regulars. Snazzy **Colle Bereto (79) (€)** *(Piazza Strozzi 5r, 055-283.156; hours: M–Sa 9AM–3AM, Su 5PM–3AM)* has great food with the drinks: salads, snacks, hot *primi*, and delectable fruit tarts. **Yab (80)** *(Via de' Sasseti 5r, 055-215.160, www.yab.it; hours: M–Sa 11:30PM–4AM)* is super-hip, with well-known DJs and good music. The trendy bar at **L'Incontro (81)** *(Savoy Hotel, Piazza della Repubblica 7, 055-273.5891, www.hotelsavoy.it; hours: 7AM–10:30AM, 12:30PM–3PM, 7:30PM–10:30PM, bar 10:30AM–1AM)* has green sofas, zebra-striped ottomans, and

leather bucket seats. Sophisticated, popular **Noir (82)** (*Lungarno Corsini 12-14r, 055-210.751; hours: 12PM–3AM*), along the Arno, is great for cocktails and *crostini*, little toasted breads. African themes at **Kilimanjaro (83)** (*Via Palazzuolo 80-82r, 055-291.661; hours: Tu–Th 7:30PM–12AM, F–Su 1PM–2AM*), from leopard-print walls to the bamboo bar, extend to tribal music though the club favors deep house. **Officina Move Bar (84)** (*Via il Prato 58r, 055-210.399; hours: Su–Th 8AM–2AM, F–Sa 8AM–3AM*), a multimedia haven, showcases hip-hop, reggae, nu-jazz, installation performances, and modern dance.

WHERE TO SHOP

Some of Florence's best shopping is in this quarter. Designer showrooms, upscale boutiques, and young designers' shops line **Via Tornabuoni (85)**, **Via della Vigna Nuova (86)**, **Via della Spada (87)**, **Piazza Strozzi (88)**, and **Via Roma (89)**. For antiques, check out **Borgo Ognissanti (90)** and **Via dei Fossi (91)**. The boutiques in **Via Porta Rossa (92)** are delightful.

Among the oldest existing pharmacies, **Officina Profumo Farmaceutica di Santa Maria Novella (94)** (*Via della Scala 16, 055-216.276, www.smnovella.it; hours: M–Sa 9:30AM–7:30PM, Su 10:30AM–7:30PM*) is famous for its soaps, perfumes, and potions, both medicinal and sensual. **Dolceforte (95)** (*Via della Scala 21, 055-219.116, www.dolceforte.it; hours: M–Sa 10AM–1PM, 3:30PM–8PM*) is known for its chocolates, marzipan, biscotti, and jams. Handmade hats and fabric toys at **Quisquilia e Pinzillacchera (96)** (*Via Palazzuolo 13r, 349-830.1973, www.pezziunici.com; hours: M 3:30PM–7PM, Tu–Sa 10AM–7PM*) are unique; provide a photo, they'll make you a portrait doll. **Fashion Room (97)** (*Via dei Palchetti 3-3A, 055-213.270, www.fashionroom.it; hours: M–F 9:30AM–1PM, 3PM–7:30PM, Sa 10AM–1PM, 3PM–6PM*) is an amazing fashion, architecture, and interior design bookstore. Women's knits and chiffons at **BP Studio (98)** (*Via della Vigna*

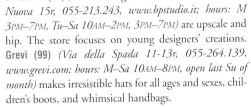

Nuova 15r, 055-213.243, www.bpstudio.it; hours: M 3PM–7PM, Tu–Sa 10AM–2PM, 3PM–7PM) are upscale and hip. The store focuses on young designers' creations. **Grevi (99)** (*Via della Spada 11-13r, 055-264.139, www.grevi.com; hours: M–Sa 10AM–8PM, open last Su of month*) makes irresistible hats for all ages and sexes, children's boots, and whimsical handbags.

Passamaneria Valmar (100) (*Via Porta Rossa 53r, 055-284.493, www.valmar-florence.com; hours: M–F 9AM–7:30PM, Sa 10AM–7:30PM*) specializes in exquisite tassels, pillows, and other trimmings in fabulous colors. **Infinity (101)** (*Borgo SS. Apostoli 18r, 055-239.8405, www.infinityfirenze.com; hours: M 2:30PM–7PM, Tu–Sa 10AM–1PM, 2:30PM–7PM, closed Aug*) produces superb handmade bags, belts, and wallets. Leather goods, straw products, and souvenirs fill the stalls at **Mercato Nuovo (102)** (*corner Via Por Santa Maria and Via Porta Rossa; hours: Apr–Oct 9AM–7PM, Nov–Mar Tu–Sa 9AM–7PM*).

Legend says if you rub the snout of Porcellino, the market's bronze boar, you'll return to Florence; for good luck, throw a coin into the water basin. **Rinascente (103)** *(Piazza della Repubblica 1, 055-219.113, www. rinascente.it; hours: M–Sa 9AM–9PM, Su 10:30AM–8PM)*, Italy's best-known department store, has something for everyone. **Ricordi Mediastore (104)** *(Via Brunelleschi 8r, 055-214.104, www.lafeltrinelli.it; hours: M–Sa 9:30AM–7:30PM, last Su of month 3PM–7:30PM)* sells DVDs, CDs, and all things music. **Eredi Chiarini (105)** *(Via Roma 16r, 055-284.478, www.eredichiarini.com; hours: M 3:30PM –7:30PM, Tu–Sa 9:30AM–7:30PM)* does well-tailored, casual-chic clothing for men and women.

WHERE TO STAY

Elegant **Hotel Montebello Splendid (106)** *(€€€–€€€€) (Via Garibaldi 14, 055-274.71, www.montebellosplendid. com)*, a 14th-century villa with a lovely internal garden and Belle Époque décor, attracts business travelers. Renaissance interiors, stained-glass ceiling, marble floors add up to opulence and refinement at **Grand Hotel (107)** *(€€€–€€€€) (Piazza Ognissanti 1, 055-271.61, www. starwoodhotels.com/luxury)*. The **Westin Excelsior (108)** *(€€€€) (Piazza Ognissanti 3, 055-271.51, www.westin. com/excelsiorflorence)* is sumptuously grand, featuring Carrara marble floors, painted ceilings, stained glass, and Neoclassical columns. More affordable in this luxury neighborhood, **Hotel Goldoni (109)** *(€–€€) (Borgo Ognissanti 8, 055-284.080, www.hotelgoldoni.com)* has comfortable rooms with charming brass beds. Clean, no-frills **Pensione Ottaviani (110)** *(€) (Piazza Ottaviani 1,*

055-239.6223, www.pensioneottaviani.it) is a cheap sleep, favored by students.

A historic monument, Hotel Aprile (111) *(€€-€€€) (Palazzo dal Borgo, Via della Scala 6, 055-216.237, www.hotelaprile.it)* charms with Renaissance antiques and worn Oriental carpets. Subdued elegance characterizes Residenza Castiglioni (112) *(€€) (Via del Giglio 8, 055-239.6013, www.residenzacastiglioni.com)*, a wonderful hotel and historic site. The likes of John Steinbeck, Barbara Bush, writers, actors, and heads of state have made Hotel Tornabuoni Beacci (113) *(€€€) (Via Tornabuoni 3, 055-212.645, www.hoteltornabuonibeacci.com)* their home-away-from-home; it's gracious, refined, and unpretentious; the terrace has a marvelous view of city rooftops. Owned by the Ferragamos, Gallery Hotel Art (114) *(€€€-€€€€) (Vicolo dell'Oro 5, 055-272.63, www. lungarnohotels.com)* is Italy's first design hotel; this super-chic, minimalist space exhibits the work of hip contemporary artists. Sophisticated Hotel Torre Guelfa (115) *(€€) (Borgo SS. Apostoli 8, 055-239.6338, www.hoteltorre guelfa.com)* is a fashionista favorite; the 13th-century tower has fantastic views while rooms have four-poster beds, marble bathrooms, and parquet floors. Hotel Helvetia and Bristol (116) *(€€€-€€€€) (Via dei Pescioni 2, 055-266.51, www.royaldemeure.com)*, the famous luxury hotel, is elegant yet subdued, and exquisitely decorated with antiques.

SANTA CROCE

Bus: 12, 13, 14, 23, A, B, C

• SNAPSHOT •

The Santa Croce district is a lively working-class community with colorful neighborhood shops, jazz clubs, theaters, and bars. The area is also known for its art restoration workshops. During Florence's disastrous November 1966 flood, the Arno rose over 19 feet above street level, resulting in enormous damage to city artworks and antiquarian books, as well as 39 deaths. The church of Santa Croce was submerged more than 16 feet—as high as the nimbus, or halo, of Jesus on its *Crucifixion* by Giovanni Cimabue. To this day, neighborhood restorers work to repair damaged sculptures, paintings, and books. The quarter retains an earthy character, despite its gentrification and fame as the home of Cibrèo, one of the city's most illustrious restaurants.

PLACES TO SEE
Landmarks:

Some of Italy's most celebrated citizens, including Niccolò Machiavelli, Michelangelo, Galileo, Lorenzo Ghiberti, and *Barber of Seville* composer Gioachino Rossini rest in the tombs of ★SANTA CROCE (117) *(Piazza Santa Croce, 055-244.619; hours: M–Sa 9:30AM–5:30PM, Su 1PM–5:30PM),* "Holy Cross," aptly nicknamed Florence's "Pantheon." This striking Gothic structure, the largest Franciscan church in the world (a reliquary within the church contains a habit said to have been worn by St. Francis himself), is a treasure trove of painting, sculpture, and architectural masterpieces. Here you'll find Cimabue's famed painting of the Crucifixion, Donatello's wooden *Crucifix*, the elegant Brunelleschi-designed Pazzi Chapel, and frescoes by Giotto and the Gaddis. A Taddeo Gaddi work in the Baroncelli Chapel, *Angel Appearing to the Shepherds*, is art history's first night scene in fresco.

TOP PICK!

Michelangelo's house, **Casa Buonarroti (118)** *(Via Ghibellina 70, 055-241.752, www.casabuonarroti.it; hours: W–M 9:30AM–2PM),* contains some of his early works and memorabilia. A 13th-century *Madonna and Child* panel by a follower of Cimabue sets the mood at serene Gothic church **San Remigio (119)** *(Piazza San Remigio, 055-284.789; hours: 9AM–12PM, 3PM–7:30PM),* located along the district's quaint medieval streets. **Museo Horne (120)** *(Via de' Benci 6, 055-244.661, www. museohorne.it; hours: M–Sa 9AM–1PM),* a 15th-century *palazzino* restored by 19th-century English architect/historian Henry Percy Horne, houses period furniture, paintings, sculpture, and Renaissance cookware.

Arts & Entertainment:

Paintings, prints, and maps at the **Museo di Firenze Com'Era (121)** *(Via dell'Oriuolo 24, 055-261.6545, www.museicivicifiorentini.it; hours: June–Sep M, Tu 9AM–2PM, Sa 9AM–7PM, Oct–May M–W 9AM–2PM, Sa 9AM–7PM)* illuminate the history and development of Florence. One of its 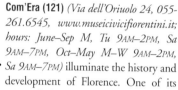 highlights is a series of Flemish lunettes (illustrations framed by arches or vaults) depicting Medici villas and gardens. One of Italy's largest theaters, **Teatro Verdi (122)** *(Via Ghibellina 91r, 055-212.320, www.teatroverdi firenze.it; call or check Web site for ticket office hours)* is known for its classical music concerts, opera and ballet performances, and other events. It has hosted Ella Fitzgerald, Frank Sinatra, Keith Jarrett, Sviatoslav Richter, Rostropovich, and Zubin Mehta, among others.

Further Afield:

To the east, in the **San Salvi** area, is the **Museo del Cenacolo di Andrea del Sarto** *(Via Andrea del Sarto 16, 055-238.8603, www.firenzemusei.it/00_english/cenacolo; hours: Tu–Su 8:15AM–1:50PM)*, housing Andrea del Sarto's *Last Supper*, one of the world's great masterpieces, and worth the trek for art aficionados.

PLACES TO EAT & DRINK
Where to Eat:

Perhaps the city's most famous restaurant, exuberant **Cibrèo (124)** (€€€€) *(Via A. del Verrocchio 8r, 055-234.1100, www.fabiopicchi.it; hours: Tu–Sa 12:50PM–2:30PM, 7PM–11PM, closed Aug, reserve ahead)* mixes traditional Tuscan and innovative cuisine. Its sister *trattoria* **Cibreino (125)** (€€) *(Via de' Macci 122r, 055-234.1100; hours: Tu–Sa 12:50PM–2:30PM, 7PM–11PM, closed Aug)* serves a limited selection of the same food at lower prices. The no-frills **Il Pizzaiuolo (126)** (€) *(Via de' Macci 113r, 055-241.171, www.ilpizzaiuolo.com; hours: M–Sa 12:30PM–2:30PM, 7:30PM–12:30AM, closed Aug)* is one of the best *pizzerie* in town. For *torta della nonna* and other luscious pastries, **La Loggia degli Albizi (127)** (€) *(Borgo degli Albizi 39r, 055-247.9574; M–Sa 7AM–8PM, closed Aug)* can't be beat. An inexpensive lunch menu and divine cappuccinos at **I Visacci (128)** (€) *(Borgo degli Albizi 80r, 055-200.1956; hours: 10AM–3AM)* are rounded out by the café's cozy atmosphere. Chocoholics must not miss **Vestri (129)** (€) *(Borgo degli Albizi 11r, 055-234.0374, www.vestri.it; hours: M–Sa 10AM–8PM, closed Aug)* for hot chocolate, chocolate confections, and chocolate ice cream. **Salumeria, Vini, Trattoria I Fratellini (130)** (€) *(Via Ghibellina 27r, 055-234.7389; hours: M–F 12PM–3:30PM, closed Aug)* is deli, wine bar, and trattoria in one; enjoy home-cooked takeout at bargain prices. By contrast, **Alle Murate (131)** (€€€€) *(Via del Proconsolo 16r, 055-240.618, www.allemurate.it;*

hours: Tu–Su 7:30PM–11:30PM) is sophisticated and romantic; nouvelle cuisine mingles with traditional Tuscan in the soft glow of candles. For classic Florentine recipes, such as *stracotto del granduca*, beef slow-cooked in Chianti with raisins, pine nuts, mint, and cinnamon, try **Dino (132)** (€€) *(Via Ghibellina 47r, 055-241.452, www.ristorantedino.it; hours: M 7:30PM–10PM, Tu–Sa 12PM–2PM, 7:30PM–10PM).*

Acqua al Due (133) (€€) *(Via della Vigna Vecchia 40r, 055-284.170, www.acquaal2.it; hours: Tu–Su 7:30PM–1AM, reserve ahead, closed 1 week in Aug)* is hip, the food is great, it's open late, and it's always packed. Its *assaggio di primi* option allows you to sample five pastas. Unpretentious **Simon Boccanegra (134)** (€€) *(Via Ghibellina 124r, 055-200.1098, www.boccanegra.com; hours: M–Sa 7PM–12AM)* pleases with traditional fare, fabulous desserts, and lively twists on local cuisine, such as tuna with sesame seeds and hot green radish, or lamb with a cocoa sauce. Its *enoteca* wine cellar next door is less expensive. **Osteria del Caffè Italiano (135)** (€€€) *(Via Isola delle Stinche 11–13r, 055-289.368, www.caffe italiano.it; hours: Tu–Su 12:30PM–1AM)* offers a Tuscan menu at mealtimes, and cheese and prosciutto between-times. Florence's most famous *gelateria*, or ice-cream parlor, **Vivoli (136)** (€) *(Via Isola delle Stinche 7r, 055-292.334, www.vivoli.it; hours: Tu–Su 8:30AM–1AM, closed 3 wks during Aug)* might just be its best. Trendy wine bar **Boccadama (137)** (€€) *(Piazza Santa Croce 25-*

26r, 055-243.640, www.boccadama.com; hours: 11AM–3PM, 6:30PM–10:30PM) also serves coffee, excellent snacks, and creative meals. Cuisine, wine, and service at three-star Michelin spot **Enoteca Pinchiorri (138)** (€€€€) (Via Ghibellina 87, 055-242.777, www.enoteca pinchiorri.it; hours: lunch Th–Sa 12:30PM–2PM, dinner W–Sa 7:30PM–10PM, closed Aug; jackets req for men) are exceptional, but prices reflect the quality (average €250). Popular **Osteria de' Benci (139)** (€€) (Via de' Benci 13r, 055-234.4923; hours: M–Sa 1PM–2:45PM, 7:45PM–10:45PM, closed 10 days during Aug) prepares pasta dishes and local favorites. Lunchtime? Try **Trattoria da Rocco (140)** (€) (inside Mercato di Sant'Ambrogio, Piazza L. Ghiberti, 339-838.4555; hours: M–Sa summer 8:30AM–3:30PM, winter 9AM–7PM, closed Aug)—tasty, quick, and inexpensive. Firenze gem **Dolci & Dolcezze (141)** (€) (Piazza Beccaria Cesare 8r, 055-234.5458; hours: Tu–Sa 8:30AM–8PM, Su 9AM–1PM, 4:30PM–7:30PM), "Sweets & Sweetness," is famed for its fruit tarts and chocolate cake (pia buona del mondo).

Bars & Nightlife:

American-style live music club **Red Garter (142)** (Via dei Benci 33r, 055-234.4904; hours: Su–Th 8:30PM–1:30AM, F–Sa 9PM–2AM) has been a hit with ex-pats and young Italians since the '60s. Trendy **Moyo (143)** (Via dei Benci 23r, 055-247.9738, www.moyo.it; hours: 6PM–2AM), the city's first wireless Internet bar, does great cocktails. On good nights, DJs spin a rocking beat at

ExMud (144) *(Corso dei Tintori 4, 055-263.8583; hours: M, Th–Sa 9PM–4AM)* that reverberates throughout its subterranean stone chambers. A mixed crowd packs the gay bar **Piccolo Caffè (145)** *(Borgo Santa Croce 23r, 055-200.1057; hours: 6:30PM–2:30AM)* on Saturdays; the bar also hosts art shows and live events. **Sèsame (146)** *(Via delle Conce 20r, 055-200.1381; hours: 7PM–late)* is an exotic nightspot: think candles, low tables, scarlet cushions, and sculpture-filled wall niches. Gay/lesbian **Yagb@r (147)** *(Via de' Macci 8r, 055-246.9022, www.yagbar.com; hours: 9PM–3AM)* is on the short list of the city's top dance-club spots; it also features video games and Internet access.

WHERE TO SHOP

If you can take your eyes off the fantastic frescoed ceilings of **Elisir (148)** *(Borgo degli Albizi 70r, 055-539.6048; hours: M 3:30PM–7:30PM, Tu–Sa 10AM–7:30PM)*, you'll be equally impressed by its perfumes, soaps, and cosmetics. Earth-friendly toys, books, and *objets* at **Cartoleria Ecologica La Tartaruga (149)** *(Borgo degli Albizi 60r, 055-234.0845; hours: M–Sa 9:30AM–7:30PM)* are made by local artisans. **Libreria Salimbeni**

(150) *(Via Matteo Palmieri 14-16r, 055-234.0904, www.libreriasalimbeni.com; hours: M–Sa 10AM–1PM, 4PM–7:30PM)* is renowned for its art books and antiquarian titles. Famous actors frequent **Filistrucchi (151)** *(Via Giuseppe Verdi 9, 055-234.4901, www.filistrucchi.it; hours: M 3PM–7PM, Tu–F 8:30AM–12:30PM,*

3PM–7PM, Sa 8:30AM–12:30PM) for wigs, masks, and special effects. Housewares and delicate home accessories at **La Bottega dei Cristalli (152)** *(Via dei Benci 51r, 055-234.4891, www.labottegadeicristalli.com; hours: 10AM–7:30PM, closed mid-Jan–mid-Feb)* range from Murano to Tuscan-made creations.

The **Mercato delle Pulci (153)** *(Piazza dei Ciompi; hours: 9AM–7:30PM)* flea market, offering everything from "junque" to true antiques, is a browser's delight. Colorful **Mercato di Sant'Ambrogio (154)** *(Piazza L. Ghiberti; hours: M–Sa 7AM–2PM)* is a cornucopia of fresh seasonal produce, cheeses, meat, fish, and pasta, plus housewares, clothing, and linens. **Sandra Dori (155)** *(Via de' Macci 103r, 348-357.4726, www.sandradori.com; hours: M–Sa 10AM–2PM, 3:30PM–7:30PM)* makes whimsical lampshades (some resembling flower-bedecked straw hats), as well as pillows, hangings, tassels, and more.

For off-the-beaten-track shopping, check out **Via Borgo La Croce** from Piazza Sant'Ambrogio to Piazza Beccaria, then **Via Gioberti**. **Mesticheria Mazzanti (156)** *(Via Borgo La Croce 101r, 055-248.0663; hours: M–Sa 8AM–1PM, 3:30PM–7:30PM, closed Aug)* is a delightful hodgepodge of housewares. **L'Elefante Verde (157)** *(Via Borgo La Croce 70–72r, 055-234.2882; hours: M–Sa 10AM–1PM, 5PM–8PM)* sells silk clothing and household items created by local artisans; custom orders taken. Inviting **Antica Officina del Farmicista Dr. Vranjes (158)** *(Via Borgo La*

*Croce 44r, 055-241.748, www.drvranjes.it; hours: M
3:30PM–7:30PM, Tu–Sa 10AM–1PM, 3:30PM–7:30PM)*
stocks essential oils; the doctor's aromatherapy practice
is on-site. East of Piazza Beccaria, you'll find a location
of Italian discount department store chain **Upim (159)**
*(Via Gioberti 70, 055-666.861, www.upim.it; hours:
9AM–8PM).*

WHERE TO STAY

Each of the three apartments at **Palazzo Bombicci Pontelli
(160)** (€€) *(Lungarno delle Grazie, 0577-907.185,
www.guicciardini.com)* offers something special: a stone
fireplace, terra-cotta details, a furnished terrace—all
with views. **Hotel River (161)** (€€) *(Lungarno della Zecca
Vecchia 18, 055-234.3529, www.hotelriver.com)*, along
the Arno, has ceiling beams, frescoes, a tropical-plant
conservatory, a terrace, and comfortable rooms. In a
12th-century palazzo, **Hotel Locanda Orchidea (162)** (€)
*(Via Borgo degli Albizi 11, 055-248.0346, www.hotel
orchideaflorence.it)* is run by a mother-daughter team
and provides clean, cozy, inexpensive accommodations;
most rooms share baths. Another budget hotel, **Hotel
Dalí (163)** (€) *(Via dell'Oriuolo 17, 055-234.0706,
www.hoteldali.com)*, located in an old palace on the cob-

blestone "Clock Road," offers
nicely furnished rooms and
free parking; some rooms have
private baths. Lovely **Locanda
de' Ciompi (164)** (€-€€) *(Via
Pietrapiana 28, 055-263.8034,
www.locandadeciompi.it)*, also

set in a former palace, is close to the popular **Mercato delle Pulci (153)** flea market *(see page 69)*. Want to know what a Florentine home is like? Consider **Le Stanze di Santa Croce (165)** (€€) *(Via delle Pinzochere 6, 055-200.1366, www.lestanzedisantacroce.com)*, a wonderful B&B with charming rooms and a welcoming terrace. The owner offers cooking classes and tours of **Mercato di Sant'Ambrogio (154)** *(see page 69)*.

chapter 2

SAN LORENZO/
SAN MARCO

FIÈSOLE

SAN LORENZO/SAN MARCO FIÈSOLE

Places to See:

1. BASILICA SAN LORENZO ★
2. Via de' Ginori
3. Palazzo Medici-Riccardi
4. Palazzo Pucci
5. Cenacolo di Sant'Apollonia
6. Chiostro dello Scalzo
7. Giardino dei Semplici
8. Santissima Annunziata
9. Spedale degli Innocenti
10. Rotonda di Santa Maria degli Angioli
11. Santa Maria Maddalena dei Pazzi
12. Tempio Israelitico
13. SAN MARCO ★
14. GALLERIA DELL'ACCADEMIA ★
15. Archeological Museum
16. Opificio delle Pietre Dure
17. Museo Stibbert
18. Teatro della Pergola
55. San Romolo
56. Sant'Alessandro
57. San Francesco
58. Villa Medici
59. San Domenico di Fièsole
60. Badia Fiesolana
61. Museo Bandini
62. Teatro Romano
63. Museo Archeologico

Places to Eat & Drink:

19. Lobs
20. Casa del Vino
21. Trattoria Zà-Zà
22. Pepò
23. Taverna del Bronzino
24. Il Vegetariano
25. Ristorante da Mimmo
26. Carabe
27. Zona 15
28. La Giostra
29. Ruth's
30. BZF (Bizzeffe)
31. Dublin Pub
33. Crisco
34. Jazz Club
64. Perseus
65. La Reggia degli Etruschi
66. India Ristorante Tandoori e Mughlai

Where to Shop:

Where to Stay:

The world is made up of five elements: earth, air, fire, water, and the Florentines.

—Pope Alexander VI

SAN LORENZO/SAN MARCO

Bus: 1, 6, 7, 10, 11, 17, 25, 31, 32, 33, C

• SNAPSHOT •

The Medici influence is everywhere in the San Lorenzo district, from the Medici Chapels, where the dynasty's greats are buried, to the family's first mansion, Palazzo Medici-Riccardi. The Medicis intended Florence to rival Rome and its buildings to last as long as, if not longer than those of the Eternal City; hence, they contracted the top art and architectural wizards of the Renaissance world. The quarter is also characterized by the bustling market surrounding the church of San Lorenzo, a vibrant pastiche of food, clothing, and knickknack vendors. A few streets away, San

Marco, the student quarter, lays claim to museums specializing in art—from antiquities to Renaissance masterpieces, from ceramics to mosaics. Its highlight: the Accademia, or Fine Arts Academy, housing Michelangelo's *David* and other works. Further east, the neighborhood around Piazza d'Azeglio becomes elegantly residential, with the nearby Sinagoga (Synagogue) and Jewish Museum adding stunning architectural and historical character to the area.

PLACES TO SEE
Landmarks:

TOP PICK!

Renaissance jewel ★**BASILICA SAN LORENZO (1)** *(Piazza San Lorenzo, 055-216.634; hours: M–Sa 10AM–5PM, Mar–Oct also Su 1:30PM–5PM)*, the Basilica of St. Lawrence, was the parish church of the Medici family. Cosimo "il Vecchio" ("the Elder") commissioned Filippo Brunelleschi to remodel the original structure, a Romanesque cathedral dating from the 11th century (which was built atop a 4th-century church consecrated by St. Ambrose). The Medici church's exterior façade was never completed due to disputes over marble; a model of Michelangelo's design for it is on display at **Casa Buonarroti** *(see page 63)*. Among the church's highlights: Brunelleschi's mini Duomo and Renaissance stylings, two bronze pulpits by Donatello, the immense fresco *The Martyrdom of St. Lawrence* by Bronzino, and Filippo Lippi's *Annunciation*. The **Medici Chapels** *(Cappelle Medicee, 055-294.883, 055-238.8602,*

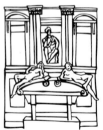

www.firenzemusei.it/medicee; hours: 8:15AM–5PM, closed 2nd & 4th Su and 1st, 3rd, & 5th M) include the Princes' Chapel *(Cappella dei Principi)*, with its mosaics, and the New Sacristy, in which you'll find Michelangelo's tomb statues *Night, Day, Dawn,* and *Dusk.* Another Michelangelo project: the Medici's **Laurentian Library** *(Biblioteca Medicea Laurenziana, Piazza di San Lorenzo 9, 055-211.590, www.bml.firenze.sbn.it; hours: M, W, F 8AM–2PM, Tu & Th 8AM–5:30PM)*, housing thousands of manuscripts and rare books. The design of its celebrated library staircase appeared to the artist in a dream, and his "blind" lobby windows influenced modern artist Mark Rothko centuries later.

A stroll along **Via de' Ginori (2)** will allow you to take in the stately homes, or *palazzi*, of the Florentine wealthy. Nearby **Palazzo Medici-Riccardi (3)** *(Via Cavour 1, 055-276.0340, www.palazzo-medici.it; hours: Th–Tu 9AM–7PM)*, the Medici family home for 100 years, was later purchased by the Riccardi family; it now houses government offices. Statues in the courtyard and frescoes in the **Cappella dei Magi**, "Chapel of the Wise Men," may be viewed by the public. **Palazzo Pucci (4)** *(Via de' Pucci 6, closed to public)* is the ancestral home of fashion designer Emilio Pucci; his forebears were allies, then enemies, of the Medici. At **Cenacolo di Sant'Apollonia (5)** *(Via XXVII Aprile 1, 055-238.8607, www.polomuseale.firenze.it/musei/apollonia; hours: 8:15AM–1:50PM, closed alternate Su & M)* you may view frescoes by Andrea del Castagno, including a stunning *Last Supper*. Nearby **Chiostro dello Scalzo (6)** *(Via Camillo Cavour 69, 055-238.8604, www.polomuseale.firenze.it/musei/chiostroscalzo; hours: M, Th, Sa 8:15AM–1:50PM or by appt)*, "Cloister of the Barefoot," refers to the Brotherhood of St. John the Baptist, whose members went shoeless in holy processions. It's lined with monochromatic frescoes by Andrea del Sarto depicting scenes from St. John's life. The Medicis cultivated medicinal and exotic plants and threw grand parties in the lovely **Giardino dei Semplici (7)** *(Via Micheli 3, 055-275.7402; hours: M–F 9AM–1PM)*, "Garden of Simples."

Frescoes by Andrea del Sarto, Pontormo, and Rosso Fiorentino grace the cloister of the church of the Holy Annunciation, **Santissima Annunziata (8)** *(Piazza della Santissima Annunziata, 055-266.181; hours: 7:30AM–12:30PM, 4PM–6:30PM)*. A tabernacle within holds a legendary painting of the Annunciation. The monk who began it felt he could not do justice to the face of the Madonna; frustrated, he fell asleep. When he awoke, he found the painting had been finished by an angel. The tabernacle shrine is laden with offerings, such as the bouquets of brides hoping for a good marriage. Across the piazza, Europe's first orphanage, **Spedale degli**  **Innocenti (9)** *(Piazza della Santissima Annunziata 12, 055-203.71, www.istituto deglinnocenti.it; hours: Th–Tu 8:30AM–2PM)*, "Hospital of the Innocents," designed by Brunelleschi, is fronted by arches decorated with terra-cotta medallions of babies by Andrea della Robbia. The octagonal **Rotonda di Santa Maria degli Angioli (10)** *(Via del Castellaccio, corner Piazza Brunelleschi and Via degli Alfani; closed to public)* was designed by Brunelleschi. Eastward, **Santa Maria Maddalena dei Pazzi (11)** *(Borgo Pinti 58, 055-247.8420; hours: 9AM–12PM, also varying times between 5PM and 7PM)*, a Baroque church, is the repository of Umbrian artist Perugino's famous fresco *Crucifixion and Saints*. **Tempio Israelitico (12)** *(Via Luigi Carlo Farini 4, 055-245.252; hours: Apr–May, Sep–Oct Su–Th Apr–Sep, Su–Th 10AM–1PM, 2PM–5PM, F 10AM–1PM; Oct–Mar, Su–Th 10AM–1PM, 2PM–4PM)*, a.k.a. the Synagogue and Jewish Museum, was built in the 1870s. It is a beautiful mix of Byzantine and Moorish architecture and decoration. The museum covers the history of Florentine Jews through objects, artifacts, photos, and drawings.

Arts & Entertainment:

★SAN MARCO (13) *(Piazza San Marco 1; church 055-287.628; hours: daily 7AM–12PM, 4PM–8PM; museum 055-238.8608, reservations 055-294.883; www.firenzemusei.it, www.polomuseale. firenze.it; hours: M–F 8:15AM–1:50PM, Sa 8:15AM–6:50PM, Su 8:15AM–7PM)*, comprising a church and a convent/monastery (now a museum) funded by Cosimo il Vecchio, was home to monk and master artist Fra Angelico, "Angelic Brother," his fellow painter Fra Bartolomeo, and reformer preacher Girolamo Savonarola. The monastery is adorned with dozens of marvelous frescoes by Fra Angelico, which provided spiritual guidance for the monks who resided here, including a resplendent *Annunciation*, a surreal *Mocking of Christ*, and a moving *Crucifixion*. You'll also see Fra Bartolomeo's famous portrait of Savonarola, as well as the living quarters and possessions of the Florentine firebrand. This is also the site of the first public library in Europe, funded by Cosimo and designed by Michelozzo.

Founded during the Renaissance, the Fine Arts Academy is among the world's first art schools. Its ★GALLERIA DELL'ACCADEMIA (14) *(Via Ricasoli 60, info 055-238.8609, call 055-294.883 for*

TOP PICK!

TOP PICK!

reservations to avoid long lines, www.firenzemusei.it, www.polomuseale.firenze.it; hours: Tu–Su 8:15AM– 6:50PM), established in 1784 by a Florentine grand

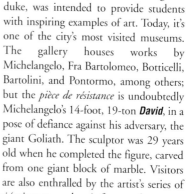

duke, was intended to provide students with inspiring examples of art. Today, it's one of the city's most visited museums. The gallery houses works by Michelangelo, Fra Bartolomeo, Botticelli, Bartolini, and Pontormo, among others; but the *pièce de résistance* is undoubtedly Michelangelo's 14-foot, 19-ton **David**, in a pose of defiance against his adversary, the giant Goliath. The sculptor was 29 years old when he completed the figure, carved from one giant block of marble. Visitors are also enthralled by the artist's series of four *Prigionieri* (prisoners or slaves), figures who appear to be struggling to free themselves from their marble backgrounds.

The **Archeological Museum (15)** *(Museo Archeologico di Firenze, Via della Colonna 38, 055-235.75, reservations: 055-294.883, www.firenzemusei.it; hours: usually M 2PM–7PM, Tu, Th 8:30AM–7PM, W, F–Su 8:30AM–2PM)* has a superb collection of Etruscan, Greek, Roman, and Egyptian antiquities. Don't miss its 4th-century BC Etruscan bronze *Chimera* (a mythical beast with three heads: those of a lion, a goat, and a serpent). **Opificio delle Pietre Dure (16)** *(Via degli Alfani 78, 055-265.11, www.opificiodellepietredure.it; hours: M–Sa 8:30AM– 12:30PM)* is a museum and workshop devoted to *pietre* *dure*, the Florentine craft of "painting in stone," creating mosaic-like artworks inlaid with marble or semiprecious gems. **Museo Stibbert (17)** *(Via Frederick Stibbert 26, 055-475.520, www.museostibbert.it; hours: M–W 10AM–2PM, ticket office closes at 1PM; F–Su 10AM–6PM, ticket office closes at 5PM)*, the villa of avid collector Frederick Stibbert, showcases the 19th-century Scot-Italian's 50-plus-room assemblage, including artworks by Botticelli, Verucchio, and Bronzino; antique porcelain; costumes; and a Hall of the Cavalcade displaying European, Islamic, and Japanese armor. Verdi, Donizetti, and Bellini all performed at **Teatro della Pergola (18)** *(Via della Pergola 18/32, 055-226.4353, www.teatrodellapergola.com; open by appointment; call for show times)*, one of Italy's oldest theaters; today it presents classical music and theater (in Italian).

PLACES TO EAT & DRINK
Where to Eat:

Lobs (19) (€€) *(Via Faenza 75r, 055-212.478, www.lobsrestaurant.com; call for hours, lunch & dinner daily)*, from *lobster*, serves fresh fish and lunch pastas. A hopping wine bar with lovely wood cabinets and marble floors, **Casa del Vino (20) (€)** *(Via dell'Ariento 16r, 055-215.609, www.casadelvino.it; hours: M–Sa 9:30AM–4:30PM, closed Sa June–Sep, closed Aug)* is great for a quick *panino* or *crostino*. Vibrant **Trattoria Zà-Zà (21) (€€)** *(Piazza Mercato Centrale 26r, 055-215.411, www.trattoriazaza.it; hours: winter M–Sa 12PM–3PM, 7PM–11PM, summer 11AM–11PM, open last Su of month)* serves regional favorites;

tourists love it. Cheery, informal **Pepò (22) (€)** *(Via Rosina 4-6r, 055-283.259, www.pepo.it; hours: 12:30PM–2:30PM, 7PM–10:30PM)* uses fresh, seasonal ingredients for its hearty, reliable meals. Elegant **Taverna del Bronzino (23) (€€€)** *(Via delle Ruote 25-27r, 055-495.220; hours: M–Sa 12:30PM–2:30PM, 7:30PM–10:30PM, closed 3 wks Aug)*, in Bronzino's 15th-century palazzo, serves fine Tuscan cuisine. **Il Vegetariano (24) (€)** *(Via delle Ruote 30r, 055-475.030, www.il-vegetariano.it; hours: Tu–F 12:30PM–2:30PM, 7:30PM–10:30PM, Sa–Su 7:30PM–10:30PM, closed 3 wks Aug)* has great food, lots of choices, ethnic dishes, and salads. You'll remember **Ristorante da Mimmo (25) (€–€€)** *(Via San Gallo 57-59r, 055-481.030, www.ristorantedamimmo.it; call for hours M–F lunch & dinner, Sa–Su dinner)*, set in a former theater, for its delicious meals and frescoed ceiling. **Carabe (26) (€)** *(Via Ricasoli 60r, 055-289.476, www.gelatocarabe.com; hours: 9AM–1AM)* specializes in fruit and nut gelato. Fashionistas pack **Zona 15 (27) (€€)** *(Via del Castellaccio 53-55r, 055-211.678; hours: M–F 11AM–3AM, Sa–Su 6PM–3AM)* for oysters and champagne at its futuristic wine bar. Warm, relaxed **La Giostra (28) (€€–€€€)** *(Borgo Pinti 12r, 055-241.341, www.ristorantelagiostra.com; hours: 12:30PM–3PM, 7:30PM–1AM)*, "The Carousel," is owned and run by a Hapsburg prince and his family. Try their pear and pecorino ravioli. Leave room for sacher torte. **Ruth's (29) (€–€€)** *(Via Luigi Carlo Farini 2A, 055-248.0888,* *www.kosheruth.com; hours: Su–Th 12:30PM–2:30PM, 7:30PM–10PM, F 12:30PM–2:30PM, Sa 7:30PM–10PM)* does kosher vegetarian, fish dishes, and Middle Eastern/North African fare, from falafel to couscous.

Bars & Nightlife:

Set in a converted medieval convent, **BZF (Bizzeffe) (30)** *(Via Panicale 61r, 055-274.1009; hours: Tu–Su 4PM–12AM, closed June–Aug)* is jazz bar, art showroom, bookshop, and Internet café in one, with coffee, tea, and yummy food. Quaff a pint of Guinness at convivial **Dublin Pub (31)** *(Via Faenza 27r, 055-274.1571, www. dublinpub.it; opens at 5PM)*, a popular Irish bar. **Crisco (33)** *(Via Sant'Egidio 43r, 055-248.0580, www. criscoclub.com/Info.html; hours: M, W–Th, Su 11AM–3AM, F–Sa 10PM–6AM)* holds parties, events, and shows X-rated videos marketed to a gay male audience. The best live jazz bar in the city, **Jazz Club (34)** *(Via Nuova de' Caccini 3, 055-247.9700, www.jazzclubfirenze.com; hours: Tu–Sa 9PM–late)* features mostly Italian but also international artists.

WHERE TO SHOP

Ida del Castillo Tessuti (35) *(Via XXVII Aprile 57-59r, 055-481.913; hours: M 3:30PM–7:30PM, Tu–Sa 9:30AM–7:30PM)* carries handmade women's clothing and accessories made of silks and velvet. Flamboyant **Mondo Albion (36)** *(Via Nazionale 121r, 055-282.451, www. mondoalbion.it; hours: M–Sa 10AM–1PM, 3:30PM–7PM)* is a shoe store like no other, selling footwear for both sexes in unique styles ranging from theatrical to wonderfully wearable. **Alice's Masks Art Studio (37)** *(Via Faenza 72r, 055-287.370, www.alicemasks.com; hours: M–Sa 9AM–1PM, 3:30PM–7:30PM)* creates fabulous papier-mâché masks known the world over. The covered market at San Lorenzo's **Mercato Centrale (38)** *(Piazza del*

Mercato Centrale, entrance on piazza and Via dell'Ariento; hours: M–Sa 7AM–2PM) features seasonal foods, meats, and cheeses. Surrounding stalls sell leather, clothes, and souvenirs. **La Ménagère (39)** *(Via de' Ginori 8r, 055-213.875; hours: M–Sa 9AM–1PM, 3:30PM–7:30PM, closed Sa PM June–Aug)* stocks Italian housewares, from handy kitchen gadgets to spiffy designer appliances. At **All'Ancora Secca (40)** *(Via de' Ginori 21r, 055-216.423; hours: M–Sa 10:30AM–1:30PM, 3PM–7:30PM, closed Sa PM June–Aug)*, hand-bound notebooks have ornate clasps, luxe leathers, and fabulous colors. The costume jewelry at

Falsi Gioielli (41) *(Via de' Ginori 34r, 055-287.237, www.falsigioielli.it; hours: M 2:30PM–7:30PM, Tu–Sa 10AM–7:30PM)*, "Fake Jewelry," is whimsical, imaginative, and always unique. **Scriptorium (42)** *(Via dei Servi 5r, 055-211.804, www.scriptoriumfirenze.com; hours: M–Sa 10AM–2PM, 3:30PM–7:30PM)* sells stationery, pens, inks, and leather boxes. Vintage costume jewelry collectors like to shop at **Oromatto (43)** *(Via dei Servi 49r, 055-216.768; hours: M–Sa 10AM–1PM, 4PM–7:30PM)*, "False

Gold;" items here date from the 1950s to the 1980s. Browse the shelves at Libreria Lef (44) *(Via Ricasoli 105-107r, 055-216.533; hours: M–F 9AM–7:30PM, Sa 9AM–1:30PM, 3:30PM–7:30PM)* for books on art, architecture, and photography, plus maps, prints, and postcards. La Botteghina (45) *(Via Guelfa 5r, 055-287.367, www.labotteghinadelceramista.it; call for hours)* presents ceramics produced by regional artisans. Farmacia SS. Annunziata (46) *(Via dei Servi 80r, 055-210.738, www.farmaciassannunziata1561.com; hours: M–Sa 9AM–1PM, 4PM–8PM)* stocks natural cosmetics and essential oils.

WHERE TO STAY

Quiet, family-run Hotel Palazzo Benci (47) (€-€€) *(Piazza Madonna degli Aldobandini 3, at Via Faenza 6r, 055-217.049/213.848, www.palazzobenci.com)* is set in a renovated 16th-century house; favored by businesspeople, it features small but comfortable rooms (with window screens, a plus during mosquito season) and a breakfast room view of the Medici Chapel. Common areas in Hotel Accademia (48) (€-€€) *(Via Faenza 7, 055-293.451, www.accademiahotel.net)* are accented by the original features of this 15th-century home of goldsmith Bernardo Cennini: stained glass, ceiling frescoes, a fireplace, and stone stairs. Atop a 19th-century palazzo, Antica Dimora Johlea (49) (€€) *(Via San Gallo 80, 055-463.3292, www.anticadimorafirenze.it)* has warm, pastel-hued rooms with canopied beds, bathrooms, Wi-Fi Internet, and access to a rooftop terrace. Its owners operate several other hotels of varying price ranges *(visit www.johanna.it)*. If God is in the details, **Hotel Il Guelfo Bianco (50)** (€€-€€€) *(Via Cavour 29, 055-288.330, www.ilguelfobianco.it)* is heaven: ceiling rafters, antique doors, and lovely bathroom tiles make this immaculate hotel memorable, as does the proprietors' art collection. *Affitta camere*, small hotels *sans* concierges, porters, or extra services, are popular choices, especially if maintained as well as **Residenza dei Pucci (51)** (€-€€) *(Via dei Pucci 9, 055-281.886, www.residenzadeipucci.com)*. Distinctive **Hotel Royal (52)** (€€) *(Via delle Ruote 50-54, 055-483.287, www.hotelroyalfirenze.it)*, once a Florentine noble's home, features a garden, inviting common spaces, and comfortable rooms. Art-filled **Palazzo Galletti (53)** (€€-€€€) *(Via Sant'Egidio 12, 055-390.5750, www.palazzogalletti.it)* is enhanced with traditional frescoes and abstract paintings, plus balconies, modern amenities, and a day spa. Elegant **Hotel Regency (54)** (€€€-€€€€) *(Piazza Massimo d'Azeglio 3, 055-245.247, www.regency-hotel.com)* is located in a beautiful residential area.

FIÈSOLE

Bus: 7 from Florence

● SNAPSHOT ●

Once a powerful Etruscan hub, the ancient hill town of Fièsole *(Tourist Office, Piazza Mino da Fièsole 36, 055-598.720, www.fiesolelifeart.it)* was defeated by Florence in the 12th century and became a wealthy Florentine suburb. The five-mile road up to Fièsole is still dotted with the villas of the rich and offers panoramic views of *Firenze*.

PLACES TO SEE
Landmarks:

The 11th-century duomo **San Romolo (55)** *(Piazza Mino da Fièsole, 055-599.566, www.cattedralefiesole.it; hours: 7:30AM–12PM, 3PM–5PM),* with its 13th-century bell tower, dominates the town's main square, once the site of a Roman forum. Within the cathedral (which has a 19th-century façade), you'll find several works of art, including a Giovanni della Robbia statue depicting St. Romulus, the town bishop to whom the duomo is dedicated.

Ascend **Via di San Francesco**, off the main square, for marvelous terrace views. Along the way, you'll pass **Sant'Alessandro (56)** *(Via S. Francesco; hours: M–Sa 10AM–12PM, 3PM–6PM, Su 3PM–6PM),* a 9th-century church with a 19th-century Neoclassical façade and

87

Roman interior columns. The **San Francesco (57)** *(Via S. Francesco 13, 055-591.75; hours: M–Sa 10AM–12PM, 3PM–6PM, Su 3PM–6PM)* friary has a tiny museum of varied artifacts and a lovely cloister. From steep **Via Vecchia Fiesolana**, take in 15th-century **Villa Medici (58)** *(Via Beato Angelico 2, 055-594.17; hours: Tu–F 9AM–1PM)*, by Michelozzo, and **San Domenico di Fièsole (59)** *(Piazza di San Domenico, 055-598.837, http://san domenicodifiesole.op.org; hours: M–F 8:30AM–12PM, 3:30PM–5PM, Sa–Su 3:30PM–5:30PM)*, where Fra Angelico took his vows. One of the artist's paintings is displayed here; it depicts the Madonna with angels and saints. Ancient **Badia Fiesolana (60)** *(Via della Badia dei Roccettini 11, 055-591.55; hours: M–F 9AM–6PM, Sa 9:30AM–12:30PM)* was Fièsole's cathedral until 1028. Its wooded surrounds are perfect for strolling.

Arts & Entertainment:

Museo Bandini (61) *(Via Dupré 1, 055-596.1293; hours: Apr–Sep 10AM–7PM, Mar, Oct 10AM–6PM, Nov–Feb W–M 10AM–2PM)* exhibits 14th- and 15th-century paintings and Luca della Robbia sculptures. Open-air **Teatro Romano (62)** *(Via Portigiani 1, 055-596.1293; call for hours, closed Tu in winter)* dates from 80 B.C.; summer concerts and plays are performed here. The ruins of two temples, Roman baths, and Etruscan walls lie beyond the theater. **Museo Archeologico (63)** *(hours: Apr–Sep 10AM–7PM, Mar, Oct 10AM–6PM, Nov–Feb W–M 10AM–2PM)*, displays Etruscan, Greek, Roman, and medieval artifacts, arranged by where they were found.

PLACES TO EAT & DRINK
Where to Eat:
Perseus (64) **(€€)** *(Piazza Mino da Fiesole 9r, 055-59.143; W–M 12PM–3PM, 7:30PM–11:30PM)* pleases the palate with regional favorites; its garden allows for warm-weather dining across from Fièsole's Roman theater. **La Reggia degli Etruschi (65)** **(€€-€€€)** *(Via S. Francesco 18, 055-59.385, www.lareggia deglietruschi.com; open for lunch and dinner)* offers views, creative *cucina toscana*, and the chance to sample some of the area's most famous wines in its *enoteca*. For a change of pace, try **India Ristorante Tandoori e Mughlai (66)** **(€-€€)** *(Largo Gramsci 43, 055-599.900; call for hours, closed Tu).*

WHERE TO STAY
Charming, family-run **Pensione Bencistà (67)** **(€€)** *(Via Benedetto da Maiano 4, 055-591.63, www.bencista.com)* offers halfboard (breakfast, dinner) or fullboard (breakfast, lunch, dinner); its terrace offers panoramic vistas. Located on a wooded hillside overlooking Florence, **Hotel Villa Fièsole (68)** **(€€-€€€)** *(Via Beato Angelico 35, 055-597.252, www.villafiesole.it)* boasts a garden, terrace, and pool. In a building with a façade designed by Michelangelo, luxurious **Villa San Michele (69)** **(€€€€)** *(Via Doccia 4, 055-567.8200, www.villasanmichele.com)* combines a forest setting, pool, and breathtaking views with an antique-bedecked interior and a cookery school.

chapter 3

OLTRARNO

OLTRARNO

Places to See:

1. San Frediano in Cestello
2. BRANCACCI CHAPEL ★
3. Santo Spirito
4. Via Maggio
5. Via de' Serragli
6. San Felice
7. PALAZZO PITTI ★
8. Boboli Gardens
9. Belvedere Fort
10. Santa Felicità
11. Via de' Bardi
12. Museo Bardini
13. Casa Siviero
14. Piazzale Michelangelo
15. San Miniato al Monte
16. Museo Zoologico La Specola

Places to Eat & Drink:

17. Ristoro di Cambi
18. Trattoria del Carmine
19. Il Guscio
20. Cavolo Nero
21. Alla Vecchia Bettola
22. Osteria Santo Spirito
23. Trattoria 4 Leoni

24. Caffè degli Artigiani
25. Filipepe
26. Onice
27. Hemingway
28. Dolce Vita
29. SottoSopra
30. Cabiria
31. Negroni
32. James Joyce

Where to Shop:

33. Antico Setificio Fiorentino
34. Brandimarte
35. Twisted
36. Ceri Vintage
37. Castorina
38. Studio Puck
39. Bartolozzi e Maioli
41. Giulio Giannini e Figlio
42. Il Torchio

Where to Stay:

43. Palazzo Magnani Feroni
44. Hotel Lungarno
45. Hotel La Scaletta
46. Hotel David

★ *Top Picks*

OLTRARNO

Bus: 6, 11, 12, 13, 23, 36, 37, D

• SNAPSHOT •

For centuries Oltrarno was the poorer section of town, until 1550 when the Medicis moved from the San Lorenzo district into the Pitti Palace. Other aristocrats soon followed "across the river" (the meaning of *Oltrarno*), building mansions along Via Maggio, on Via de' Serragli, and around Piazza Santo Spirito. Today, this lovely Bohemian area is full of artisans' workshops, run-down *botteghe*, antique shops, palazzi, artists, and working-class locals. Here you will find the authentic Florence. Off Ponte Vecchio, Palazzo Pitti and the beautiful Boboli Gardens sprawl down the middle of Oltrarno. East of Ponte Vecchio along the river, San Niccolò buzzes with *osterie* and wine bars. To the south a hill rises with marvelous winding roads leading to Piazzale Michelangelo and San Miniato al Monte, offering marvelous views of the city.

PLACES TO SEE
Landmarks:

The dome of **San Frediano in Cestello (1)** (*Piazza di Cestello, 055-215.816; hours: M–F 9AM–12PM, 4:30PM–5PM, Su 4:30PM–7:30PM*), a late-17th-century Baroque church, stands out across the city skyline. In the church of Santa Maria del Carmine, the

★**BRANCACCI CHAPEL (2)** (*Piazza del Carmine, 055-238.2195; hours: M–Sa 10AM–5PM, Su 1PM–5PM, reservation required, 15-minute visits only*) is famous for the twelve frescoes painted in the 15th century by Masolino, his protégé Masaccio, and Filippino Lippi. Masaccio's realistic and highly emotional renderings were avant-garde in his day and contrasted in their simplicity to his teacher Masolino's more decorative, courtly style. Masaccio died at the age of 27; his work on the frescoes was completed by Lippi several decades later. The frescoes focus on the life of St. Peter and the theme of redemption. Great artists, including Leonardo, have studied Masaccio's *oeuvre* in the Brancacci Chapel.

One of Florence's most beautiful churches, **Santo Spirito (3)** (*Piazza Santo Spirito, 055-210.030; hours: Th–Tu 8AM–12PM, 4PM–6PM, W 8AM–12PM*) spans several eras: the foundation is 13th-century; the church, Brunelleschi's 1435 design; the altar, 17th-century Baroque; and the façade, 18th-century. Tall colonnaded aisles, coffered ceilings, and Renaissance works by Ghirlandaio, Lippi, and Rosselli, among others, add to the magnificent edifice. Next door, the refectory, called the **Cenacolo**, displays Gothic and Romanesque art. Wander the neighborhood streets, from the furniture restorers' studios in **Piazza Santo Spirito** to the majestic palaces of **Via Maggio (4)** and **Via de' Serragli (5)**. Pop into **San Felice (6)** (*Piazza San Felice; hours: 9AM–12PM, 4PM–7PM*) to see Ghirlandaio's *Madonna* and the *Crucifix*, by the school of Giotto.

★**PALAZZO PITTI (7)** *(Piazza Pitti, 055-294.883, www.firenzemusei.it, www.polo museale.firenze.it; hours: open daily at 8:15AM, various closing times throughout the year; Palatine Gallery & Royal Apartments closed M),* built for the banker Luca Pitti, became the main Medici residence in

1550. Today, it is a group of museums housing the Medici treasures. Highlights include the **Palatine Gallery**, with myriad masterpieces, many of which are Raphael paintings; **Museo degli Argenti**, with silver, gold, crystal, *pietre dure*, ivory, and amber; the magnificent, ornate **Royal Apartments**; and the Ammanati-designed inner **courtyard**. The palace's splendid formal **Boboli Gardens (8)** *(Piazza Pitti, 055-265.1838; hours: June–Sep 8:15AM–7:30PM, Apr–May, Oct 8:15AM–6:30PM; Nov–Feb 8:15AM–4:30PM; Mar 8:15AM–5:30PM)* incorporate, among other features, the **Amphitheatre**, where the world's first opera performances were held; the **Grotta Grande**, a riotous conglomeration of statuary and architecture; the **Orangery**, a greenhouse; the moat and garden with Giambologna's **Oceanus Fountain**; the **Viottolone**, a colonnade of cypresses and statues; the **Costume Gallery** and **Porcelain Museum**; and the **Belvedere Fort (9)** *(Via San Leonardo, 055-276.81; call for hours)*, affording spectacular views.

The main attraction at **Santa Felicità (10)** *(Piazza Santa Felicità, 055-213.018; hours: 8AM–12PM, 3:30PM–6:30PM)* are the Pontormos, especially *The Deposition* and *Annunciation*. Small **Via de' Bardi (11)** is interesting for the stern façades of palaces with beautiful courtyard gardens. **Museo Bardini (12)** *(Piazza de' Mozzi 1, 055-234.2427/294.883, www.polomuseale.firenze.it; closed for restoration, call for update)* houses antique furniture, artwork, musical instruments, ceramics, and armor. **Casa Siviero (13)** *(Lungarno Serristori 1-3, 055-234.5219, www.museocasasiviero.it; hours: Oct–May, Sa 10AM–6PM; June–Sep Sa 10AM–2PM, 3PM–7PM; all year Su, M 10AM–1PM)* was the home of secret agent Rodolfo Siviero, famed for his recovery of Nazi-plundered Italian art masterpieces.

The spectacular view of Florence and the Arno from **Piazzale Michelangelo (14)** is famous. Here, you can also see a bronze replica of Michelangelo's *David*. Walk there, taking Via San Niccolò, Via San Miniato, and Via del Monte alle Croci, to appreciate the beautiful villas and gardens along the way. **San Miniato al Monte (15)** *(Via delle Porte Sante 34, 055-234.2731; call for hours)*, a Romanesque church, was built on the site of a shrine to the martyr St. Minias. Legend has it that after being decapitated in the third century for his Christian beliefs, he picked up his severed head and walked with it from the Arno to this spot on the hill. White Carrara and green Verde di

Prato marble inlays decorate the façade while the remarkable interior has mosaics, Roman columns, fading frescoes, terra-cotta roundels, and intarsia work.

Arts & Entertainment:

Museo Zoologico La Specola (16) *(Via Romana 17, 055-228.8251, www.msn.unifi.it; hours: Tu–Sa 9:30AM–4:30PM, Su 9:30AM–6PM)*, a zoological and anatomical museum, has gruesome wax models of dissected diseased corpses and pictures of the city during the plague. In summer, films are shown in the open air at **Belvedere Fort (9)** *(see page 94, www.ateliergroup.it; call for hours)*.

PLACES TO EAT & DRINK
Where to Eat:

Ristoro di Cambi (17) (€€) *(Via San Onofrio 1r, 055-217.134, www.anticoristorodicambi.it; hours: M–Sa 12:15PM–2:30PM, 7:30PM–10:30PM)*, with vaulted ceiling, bare brick, old photos, and excellent Tuscan cuisine, is a local favorite. **Trattoria del Carmine (18)** (€-€€) *(Piazza del Carmine 18r, 055-218.601, www.florence. ala.it/carmine; hours: M–Sa 12PM–2:30PM, 7:30PM–10:30PM, closed 3wks Aug)* serves good Tuscan home cooking in a warm, family ambience. The menu at no-frills **Il Guscio (19)** (€€) *(Via dell'Orto 49, 055-224.421, www.ristoranteilgusciofirenze.com, www.il-guscio.it; hours: Tu–Sa 8PM–11PM, closed Aug)* is eclectic: try ricotta ravioli in eggplant ricotta sauce, gnocchi with asparagus crepes, beef filet with truffles, or mixed seafood in tomato sauce. Elegant, intimate **Cavolo Nero (20)** (€€) *(Via dell'Ardiglione 22, 055-294.744, www.cavolonero.it;*

call for hours, lunch & dinner daily) is a gastronomic find—Tuscan cuisine with a sophisticated twist: leek and almond crepe; lamb ribs in bread crust with roasted potatoes and spiced figs marmalade; roasted cod with onion fondue; and the fabulous warm chocolate tart, *tenerina di cioccolata fondente*. **Alla Vecchia Bettola (21)** **(€-€€)** *(Viale Vasco Pratolini 317, 055-224.158, www.allavecchiabettola.com; hours: Tu–Sa 12PM–2:30PM, 7:30PM–10:30PM)*, a top spot for traditional Florentine cuisine, garners popularity from its good food and lively atmosphere. One of the hippest restaurants this side of the Arno, **Osteria Santo Spirito (22) (€€)** *(Piazza Santo Spirito 16r, 055-238.2383; hours: 12:45PM–2:30PM, 8PM–12AM)* attracts writers, journalists, and artists with its innovative cuisine; dance music takes over at night. **Trattoria 4 Leoni (23) (€€)** *(Via dei Vellutini 1r, 055-218.562, www.4leoni.com; hours: M–Tu, Th–Su 12PM–2:30PM, 7PM–11PM, W 7PM–11PM)*, a rustic-turned-trendy trattoria, serves upscale versions of Tuscan cuisine. For a light snack or if you yearn for a country inn, **Caffè degli Artigiani (24) (€)** *(Via dello Sprone 16r, 055-291.882, www.firenze-oltrarno.net/caffeartigiani; hours: M–Sa 9AM–11PM)* is a beautiful, inviting café. **Filipepe (25) (€€)** *(Via di San Niccolò 39r, 055-200.1397, www.filipepe.com; hours: 7:30PM–1AM, closed 2 wks Aug)*, hip, quirky, and affordable, presents eye-catching combinations of delicious foods, like beef *carpaccio* with caciocavallo cheese, ginger, oil and lemon, or *Pici* pasta with fresh crab and asparagus; the desserts are sinful. Michelin-starred **Onice (26) (€€€€)** *(Hotel Villa La Vedetta, Viale Michelangelo 78, 055-681.631,* *www.villalavedettahotel.com; hours: 12:30PM–2:30PM, 7:30PM–11PM)* presents light lunches and exceptional

Italian-Asian fusion dinners; the view is fabulous. Whether resting from a visit to the **Brancacci Chapel (2)** *(see page 93)* or stopping for after-dinner coffee and sweets, you can't go wrong with **Hemingway (27)** (€-€€) *(Piazza Piattellina 9r, 055-284.781, www.hemingway.fi.it; hours: M–Th 4:30PM–1AM, F–Sa 4:30PM–2AM, Su 3:30PM–1AM)*: from homemade ice cream and biscotti to Vinsanto and warm chocolate chip cookies, it hits the spot.

Bars & Nightlife:

Dolce Vita (28) *(Piazza del Carmine, 055-284.595, www.dolcevitaflorence.com; hours: Apr–Oct daily 5PM–2AM, Nov–Mar Tu–Su 5PM–2AM)* is the granddaddy of hip Florentine bars; sink into a sofa under a sparkly crystal lamp or mingle with the crowds on the piazza. At **SottoSopra (29)** *(Via dei Serragli 48r, 055-282.340; hours: M–Sa 7PM–2AM, closed June–Sep)* the DJs keep the music coming while friendly Florentines practice their English on you. Candlelight and mellow jazz create mood at **Cabiria (30)** *(Piazza Santo Spirito 4r, 055-215.732; hours: M, W–Su 8AM–1:30AM)*, a trendy gathering spot on this popular piazza. Very cool, with black and red interior, **Negroni (31)** *(Via dei Renai 17r, 055-243.647, www.negronibar.com; hours: M–Sa 8AM–2AM, Su 6:30PM–2AM, closed 2 wks Aug)* mounts art and photo exhibits; the music is among the latest releases of progressive bands. Lively and friendly, **James Joyce (32)** *(Lungarno Benvenuto Cellini 1r, 055-658.0856; hours: M–Th 6PM–2AM, F–Su 6PM–3AM)* must be the best pub in the city; its big garden is an asset.

WHERE TO SHOP

Oltrarno is where artisans traditionally lived and worked. You'll find plenty of antiques stores along **Via Maggio (4)**. For fine antiques, you might try **Campolmi** *(Via Maggio 5, 055-295.367; call for hours)*; **Traslucido** *(Via Maggio 9r, 055-212.750, www.traslucido.it)*; **Pratesi** *(Via Maggio 13, 055-239.6568)*; **Gallori-Turchi** *(Via Maggio 14r, 055-282.279; call for hours)*; **Guido Bartolozzi Antichità** *(Via Maggio 18r, 055-215.602; www.guidobartolozzi.com; call for hours)*; or **Zecchi** *(Via Maggio 34r, 055-293.368)*. Opulent fabrics straight from Renaissance paintings can be found at **Antico Setificio Fiorentino (33)** *(Via L. Bartolini 4, 055-213.861, www.anticosetificiofiorentino.com; hours: M–F 9AM–1PM, 2PM –5PM, by appt)*, purveyors to the Kremlin and royal palaces; goods include curtains, bedspreads, boxes, trimmings, and scarves. **Brandimarte (34)** *(Viale L. Ariosto 11Cr, 055-230.41/411/4120, www.brandimarte.com; hours: M–F 9AM–1PM, 2PM–7PM, Sa 9AM–1PM, 3PM–7PM)* hammers out handmade objects in silver, from decorative pieces to silverware, jewelry, and desk accessories. **Twisted (35)** *(Borgo San Frediano 21r, 055-282.011; hours: M–Sa 9AM–12:30PM, 3PM–7:30PM)* boasts all things jazz: CDs, DVDs, books, posters, scores. It's mostly women's clothes, shoes, and costume jewelry at **Ceri Vintage (36)** *(Via dei Serragli 26r, 055-217.978; hours: M–Sa 9:30AM–12:30PM, 3:30PM–7PM)*, which also carries vintage military uniforms, toys, and posters.

Wood-carved moldings, ornaments, and architectural objects at **Castorina (37)** *(Via Santo Spirito 36r, 055-212.885, 055-265.0505, www.castorina.net; hours: M–F 9AM–1PM, 3:30PM–7:30PM, Sa 9AM–1PM, closed Aug)* make wonderful gifts. **Studio Puck (38)** *(Via Santo Spirito 28r, 055-280.954, www.studiopuck.it; hours: M–F 9AM–7PM, Sa 9:30AM–1PM)* produces hand-colored engravings in beautiful wooden frames. The wood carvings of **Bartolozzi e Maioli (39)** *(Via dei Vellutini 5, 055-281.723, www.bartolozziemaioli.it; hours: M–Sa 9AM–1PM, 3:30PM–7PM, closed Aug)* are stunning; their restoration work, famous. **Giulio Giannini e Figlio (41)** *(Piazza Pitti 37r, 055-212.621, www.giuliogiannini.it; hours: M–Sa 10AM–7:30PM, Su 10:30AM–6:30PM)* is an old-fashioned paper shop, with desk accessories and fabulous marbled books, journals, stationery, and other paper goods. For

handmade paper boxes, stationery, and albums, try **Il Torchio (42)** *(Via dei Bardi 17, 055-234.2862, www.legatoriailtorchio.com; hours: M–F 9:30AM–1:30PM, 2:30PM–7PM, Sa 9:30AM–1PM)*, or just watch the bookbinders at their craft.

WHERE TO STAY

Magnificent and sedate, with a sumptuous courtyard, Palazzo Magnani Feroni (43) (€€€-€€€€) *(Borgo San Frediano 5, 055-239.9544, www.palazzomagnani feroni.com)* makes you feel like you're in a private mansion, not a hotel. Luxurious riverside Hotel Lungarno (44) (€€€-€€€€) *(Borgo San Jacopo 14, 055-272.61, www. lungarnohotels.com)* blends modern and classic in elegant rooms and boasts a superb art collection of 20th-century masters. Just past Ponte Vecchio, Hotel La Scaletta (45) (€-€€) *(Via Guicciardini 13, 055-283.028 or 055-214.255, www.hotellascaletta.it)*, an old-fashioned hotel, has a heart-stopping view of Pitti Palace, Boboli Gardens, and even Fièsole from the roof garden. Small, charming Hotel David (46) (€€€) *(Viale Michelangelo 1, 055-681.1695, www.davidhotel.com)* seems like a friendly private home.

Part II: Tuscany

While Florence is a testament to the genius, drama, and intrigue that spawned the most magnificent period in the history of Western art and culture, Tuscany makes you savor the here and now through both the extraordinary natural bounty of the land and the serene, leisurely pace of life. Named after the Etruscans, who settled in the region in the 8th century B.C. and were later conquered by the Romans, Tuscany is full of ancient artifacts, both in museums and in town ruins. A rich history characterized by inter-state rivalries has left Tuscany dotted with fortress towns and churches, and its share of magnificent art, medieval architecture, and dramatic history.

But it is another quality altogether that enchants in Tuscany, one that could be called simple natural splendor. Hills and woods, mountains and seas, rocky crags and hot springs—Tuscany has them all. It is as if some primeval alchemy is at work in nature here, with the way the sun and rolling hills turn light into gold; the way majestic cypress trees, lined up like green soldiers along a ridge, nudge us to pay attention to our surroundings, to their smells, sounds, and tastes; the way the slope of the hills makes us stop to admire, take our time, and enjoy the breeze. Savor the aroma of freshly picked tomatoes, the taste of extra-virgin olive oil, the pungency of a pecorino cheese, the smoothness of full-bodied wine. The region is renowned for its cuisine, and virtually every area has its local products—wine, beef, olive oil. The land vibrates with the colors of the harvest: greens, ambers, golds, reds.

It is the acknowledgment and appreciation of beauty that enchants in Tuscany, with its unapologetic recognition of something both human and divine in the aesthetic glories of the land. While human rivalries created a turbulent history throughout the province and fostered fierce loyalty within each town and village, they also endowed each regional district with the particular flavor that characterizes it to this day. The best way to experience this *anima* is to focus on one or two provinces of Tuscany, savoring them in depth, rather than trying to cover the entire region.

chapter 4

LUCCA, PISA, AND
NORTHWESTERN
TUSCANY

LUCCA, PISA, AND NORTHWESTERN TUSCANY

A. LUCCA ★
B. MONTECATINI TERME
C. PISTOIA
D. PRATO
E. CARRARA

F. VIAREGGIO & VERSILIA RIVIERA
G. PISA ★
H. SAN MINIATO
I. LIVORNO

• SNAPSHOT •

Northwestern Tuscany offers a diversity of natural, artistic, architectural, and cultural sights. Historic landmarks, churches, and museums make cities like Lucca, Pisa, Prato, and Pistoia worthwhile destinations. The Apuan Alps in the Garfagnana and Lunigiana areas to the north offer parks, forests, and beautiful hiking terrain. To the west, the seashore of the Versilia Riviera stretches to Viareggio, a popular beach resort town, and Torre del Lago Puccini, where the composer Puccini wrote most of his operas.

Places to See:

1. Ramparts
2. Duomo di San Martino
3. Museo della Cattedrale
4. San Giovanni e Reparata
5. San Michele in Foro
6. Casa Natale di Puccini
7. Museo Nazionale di Palazzo Mansi
8. Santa Maria Corteorlandini
9. Palazzo Pfanner
10. San Frediano
11. Torre Guinigi
12. Santa Maria Forisportam
13. Museo Nazionale di Villa Guinigi
14. Teatro del Giglio

Places to Eat & Drink:

15. La Buca di Sant'Antonio
16. Trattoria Da Leo
17. Locanda di Bacco
18. Locanda Buatino
19. Osteria Baralla
20. Ristorante Puccini
21. Antico Caffè di Simo
22. Gelateria Veneta
23. Gelateria Sergio Santini
24. Pasticceria Taddeucci
25. Rewine Bar
26. Vinarkia

Where to Shop:

27. Via Fillungo
28. Via Vittorio Veneto
29. Via Santa Croce
30. Via dei Bacchettoni
31. Piazza San Martino
32. Piazza San Giusto
33. Mercato del Carmine
34. Carli
35. Cacioteca
36. L'Incontro
37. Enoteca Vanni

Where to Stay:

38. San Frediano Guest House
39. La Romea
40. Palazzo Alexander
41. Piccolo Hotel Puccini
42. La Boheme

Vle. P. Baroni

16

Pzle. de Martiri

N

Vle. Carlo del Prete

Pass. delle Mura Urbane

V. di Salicchi

V. Michele Rosi

V. del Fosso

0   0.125 mi
0   125 m

30

San Francesco

13

V. della Quarquonia

V. del Mezzo

V. Busdraghi

V. Recchioni

Vle. dei

V. di Borgo

Pza. S. Maria del Borgo

35

V. del Carrozieri

V. Santa Gemma Galgani

S. Pietro Somaldi

26

Pza. San Francesco

V. Bruneto Pacii

V. Santa Chiara

V. Elisa

V. della Zecca

Pza. S. Pietro

V. di Fratta

V. del Fosso

V. San Nicolao

V. San Micheletto

V. della Cavalleria

V. Fillungo

19

Pza. del Anfiteatro

V. dell'Angelo Custode

10

Pza. del Collegio

Pza. San Frediano

V. Cesare Battisti

27

V. Antonio Mordini

11

V. del Guinigi

Pza. Maria Foris Portam

12

V. del Giardino Botanico

San Agostino

9

38

V. del Carmine

Pza. S. Agostino

17

34

21

V. Santa Croce

V. della Rosa

29

V. dell'Arcivescovo

V. del Fosso

V. di Poggia

V. San Giorgio

8

16

37

42

22

Torre del Ore

Pza. dei Servi

V. S. Vallisneri

Pza. San Bernardino

3

V. del Moro

San Salvatore

Pza. de S. Salvatore

V. Santa Giustina

25

5

24

Roma

2

V. del Battisteto

40

V. Galli Tassi

20

11

Pza. San Michele

4

11

Pza. S. Martino

6

V. Vittorio Veneto

Vle. Regina Margherita

V. San Paolino

23

15

32

Pass. delle Mura Urbane

7

Pza. Napoleone

Pza. del Giglio

14

Vle. Gen. Marti Diani

Bastione San Colombano

V. San Paolino

V. Vittorio Emanuele

San Romano

Palazzo Ducale

28

Corso Garibaldi

Porta S. Pietro

V. E. Cialdi

1

Vle. Regina Margherita

Train Station

107

A city colonized by ancient Rome in 180 B.C., Lucca is a lovely, lively town, popular among both Italian and foreign visitors. In a harmonious mix of Romanesque, Gothic, and Renaissance architecture, narrow streets follow the old Roman street plan and beautiful old storefronts retain their original grace. A lovely walkway dotted with trees and grass rims the red brick

Renaissance ramparts. This is where you'll find the *Lucchesi* at their favorite pastime, the *passeggiata*, or evening stroll. Many streets in Lucca are pedestrian walkways, so footing it or biking is preferable. There are also many lovely villas and gardens that dot the countryside around Lucca—check the tourist office for short excursion suggestions and itineraries.

Tourist Info: Comune di Lucca Tourist Office (*Piazzale Giuseppe Verdi, near Vecchia Porta San Donato, 0583-442.944; hours: 9AM–7PM*); APT (*Piazza Santa Maria 35, 0583-919.931; www.luccaturismo.it; call for hours*). Other tourist offices are located at Porta Elisa, Viale Luporini, and in Palazzo Ducale. For more info visit *www.luccavirtuale.it.*

PLACES TO SEE
Landmarks, Arts & Entertainment:
The 16th-century **Ramparts (1)** encircling the city constitute a public park 2.5 miles around, with lovely views of the town and surroundings. Walk the ramparts or bike around the walls. Rent bikes at **Cicli Bizzarri** (*Piazza*

Santa Maria 32, 0583-496.682, www.ciclibizzarri.net; call for hours), **Antonio Poli** *(Piazza Santa Maria 42, 0583-493.787, www.biciclettepoli.com; call for hours),* or at other shops in the square.

The marvelous **Duomo di San Martino (2)** *(Piazza San Martino, 0583-957.068; hours: Su–F 9:30AM–5:45PM, Sa 9:30AM–6:45PM),* with its arcades, tiered colonnades, intricate decorations, and fabulous marble inlays, is a superb example of Pisan-Romanesque architecture. Its 13th-century façade was plastered to an existing *campanile,* or bell tower. Highlights include Tintoretto's *Last Supper,* Matteo Civitali's marble *Tempietto,* and inside this octagonal bapistry, the *Volto Santo,* a wooden crucifix said to have been begun by Christ's follower Nicodemus and finished by angels. Jacopo della Quercia's exquisite tomb of Ilaria, wife of Lucca's early 15th-century *capo* Paolo Guinigi, is in the Sacristy.

The **Museo della Cattedrale (3)** *(Piazza Antelminelli 5, 0583-490.530, www.museocattedralelucca.it; hours: mid-Mar–Oct 10AM–6PM, Nov–mid-Mar M–F 10AM–3PM, Sa–Su 10AM–6PM)* houses treasures from the Duomo: sculpture, gold and silver, and masterpieces such as della Quercia's *Apostle* and Vincenzo di Michele's *Croce di Pisani.* **San Giovanni e Reparata (4)** *(Piazza San Giovanni, Via del Duomo, 0583-490.530; hours same as Museo della Cattedrale)* was built on the ruins of a Roman house and baths; visit the excavations, and don't miss the church's marvelous ceiling. **San Michele in Foro (5)** *(Piazza San Michele, 0583-484.59; hours: 7:30AM–*

12PM, 3PM–6PM) is situated in what was the ancient Roman forum in 180 B.C. It rivals the Duomo in exuberance, with twisted columns and Cosmati work (inlaid marble) across the façade. Wild animals and fantasmagoric creatures seem to leap from the stone.

Casa Natale di Puccini (6) *(Corte San Lorenzo 8/9, off Via di Poggio, 0583-584.028; hours: Nov–May Tu–Su 10AM–1PM, 3PM–6PM, June–Sep 10AM–6PM, closed Oct)*, the composer's birthplace, contains interesting memorabilia of the work and life of Lucca's musical genius. The beautiful **Museo Nazionale di Palazzo Mansi (7)** *(Via Galli Tassi 43, 0583-555.70; hours: Tu–Sa 8:30AM–7PM, Su 8:30AM–1PM)* houses mostly 17th-century paintings and furnishings. Flamboyantly Baroque, **Santa Maria Corteorlandini (8)** *(Via Santa Maria Corteorlandini 10/A, 0583-467.464; hours: 8:30AM–12PM, 4PM–6PM)* is full of color, gilt, and *trompe l'oeil* frescoes.

Palazzo Pfanner (9) *(Via degli Asili 33, 0583-954.029, www.palazzopfanner.it; hours: Apr–Oct 10AM–6PM)* is known for its exquisite gardens (seen in the film *The Portrait of a Lady*), gorgeous staircase, and galleries. When Fredian, a 6th-century Irish monk, saved Lucca by "diverting" the River Serchio, he became bishop, and eventually a saint. Six centuries later, **San Frediano (10)** *(Piazza San Frediano, 0583-493.627; hours: Apr–mid-Nov M–Sa 7:30AM–12PM, 3PM–5PM, Su 10:30AM–5PM)* was built in his memory with a mosaic façade that looks Byzantine. Climb the 144-foot-high **Torre Guinigi (11)** *(Via Sant'Andrea at Via Chiave d'Oro, 0583-485.24 or*

0583-491.205, hours: Mar–May 9AM–7:30PM, June–Sep 15 9AM–12AM, Sep 16–Oct 9:30AM–8PM, Nov–Feb 9:30AM–5:30PM), and you'll be rewarded with a fabulous view of Lucca and the countryside from the roof garden.

Santa Maria Forisportam (12) *(Piazza Santa Maria Forisportam, 0583-467.769; hours: M–Sa 9AM–12PM, 3:15PM–6:30PM)*, originally outside the Roman walls *(forisportam)*, has an unfinished façade with beautiful carvings. Once Paolo Guinigi's mansion, the **Museo Nazionale di Villa Guinigi (13)** *(Via della Quarquonia, 0583-496.033; hours: Tu–Sa 9AM–7PM, Su 9AM–2PM)* houses sculpture, paintings, furniture, and architectural pieces. **Teatro del Giglio (14)** *(Piazza del Giglio 13/15, 0583-467.521 and 0583-465.320, www.teatrodelgiglio.it)* holds concerts year-round and opera (favoring Puccini) from mid-November to mid-March.

PLACES TO EAT & DRINK
Where to Eat:

Classy, charming, and unpretentious, **La Buca di Sant'Antonio (15)** **(€€-€€€)** *(Via della Cervia 3, 0583-558.81, www.bucadisantantonio.com; hours: Tu–Sa 12:30PM–3PM, 7:30PM–10PM, Su 12:30PM–3PM)* could be Lucca's best restaurant, offering delicious Tuscan cuisine in a lovely 18th-century palazzo. **Trattoria Da Leo (16)** **(€)** *(Via Tegrimi 1, 0583-492.236, www.trattoriadaleo.it;*

hours: 12PM–2:30PM, 7:30PM–10:30PM) has singing waiters and great home-made pastas. Hip, popular **Locanda di Bacco (17)** (€€) *(Via San Giorgio 36, 0583-493.136, www.locandadibocco.it; hours: W–M 12:30PM–2:30PM, 7:30PM–10:30PM, book ahead)* has a great wine list and interesting food: *crostini* with gorgonzola and honey, *pappardelle* with wild boar. **Locanda Buatino (18)** (€) *(Borgo Giannotti 508, near Piazzale Martiri della Libertà, 0583-343.207; hours: M–Sa 12PM–2PM, 7:30PM–10PM, closed 2 wks Aug, book ahead)*, relaxed but cosmopolitan, serves homemade pasta and excellent meat and fish dishes at communal tables; on Mondays, from October to May, jazz is the added feature. Snug in a medieval palazzo, **Osteria Baralla (19)** (€–€€) *(Via Anfiteatro 5/7/9, 0583-440.240; call for hours, closed Su, book ahead)*, with its vaulted ceilings, has charm galore; the food is good, typical local fare. **Ristorante Puccini (20)** (€€–€€€) *(Corte San Lorenzo 1-2, 0583-316.676, www.ristorantepuccini.it; hours: Th–M 12:30PM–2:30PM, 7:30PM–10:30PM, Tu–W 7:30PM–10:30PM)*, Lucca's best fish place, is in a serene courtyard; its tasting menus include meat or fish. Italian artists and writers, including Puccini, Verdi, and Leopardi, made **Antico Caffè di Simo (21)** (€) *(Via Fillungo 58, 0583-496.234, www.caffedisimo.it; hours: Apr–Oct 8AM–12AM, Nov–Mar Tu–Su 8AM–8:30PM)* famous; its 1846 ambience continues to delight, as do the pastries, gelato, and savory dishes.

For fabulous ice cream, go to legendary **Gelateria Veneta (22)** (€) *(Chiasso Barletti 23, 0583-493.727, www. gelateriaveneta.net; hours:10AM–1AM)*; or try **Gelateria Sergio Santini (23)** (€) *(Piazza Cittadella 1, 0583-552.95, www.gelateria santini.it; hours: summer 9AM–12AM, winter Tu–Su 9AM–9PM)*; its iced panettone *(panettone gelato)* is divine. Famous **Pasticceria Taddeucci (24)** (€) *(Piazza San Michele 34, 0583-494.933, www.taddeucci.com; hours: F–W 8AM–1PM, 3:30PM–8PM)* makes marvelous cakes, tarts, and nutty cookies like *cantucci* and *panforte*.

Bars & Nightlife:

Rewine Bar (25) *(Via Calderia 6, 0583-050.124; call for hours, closed Su)* is a good, friendly wine bar. **Vinarkia (26)** *(Via Fillungo 188, 0583-495.336; call for hours)* does wine tastings and has a free buffet daily.

WHERE TO SHOP

Lucca's main shopping streets are Via Fillungo (27) (designer boutiques), Via Vittorio Veneto (28), and Via Santa Croce (29). Lucca's **market**, selling clothes, house-wares, food, and flowers, is on Via dei Bacchettoni (30) *(W, Sa 8AM–12:30PM)*. The **antiques market** is in Piazza San Martino (31) *(3rd weekend each month)* and the **crafts market** is in Piazza San Giusto (32) *(last weekend of month)*. Mercato del Carmine (33) *(off Piazza del Carmine; hours: 8AM–12PM, 4PM–7:30PM)*, with its lovely colonnades, sells fresh regional produce.

The frescoed vaults at **Carli (34)** *(Via Fillungo 95, 0583-491.119; call for hours)* are as dazzling as the antique jewelry, silver, and watches. At **Cacioteca (35)** *(Via Fillungo 242, 0583-496.346; hours: M–Sa 8AM–1:15PM,*

3:30PM–8:15PM) cheese reigns. For housewares, porcelain, and ceramics, **L'Incontro (36)** *(Via Buia 9, off Via Fillungo, 0583-491.225; call for hours)* is the place. **Enoteca Vanni (37)** *(Piazza del Salvatore 7, 0583-491.902, www.enotecavanni.com; call for hours)*, specializing in wines and olive oil, offers tastings and lessons.

WHERE TO STAY

San Frediano Guest House (38) *(€)* *(Via degli Angeli 19, 0583-469.630, www.sanfrediano.com)*, a comfortable B&B, is off the chic Via Fillunga. **La Romea (39)** *(€€)* *(Vicolo delle Ventaglie 2, 0583-464.175, www.laromea.com)*, in a 14th-century palazzo, has special touches: antique furniture, beams, and parquet floors. **Palazzo Alexander (40)** *(€€-€€€)* *(Via Santa Giustina 48, 0583-583.571, www.palazzoalexander.it)*, a small boutique hotel, is intimate, romantic, and ornately Venetian. **Piccolo Hotel Puccini (41)** *(€)* *(Via di Poggio 9, 0583-554.21, www.hotelpuccini.com)* is charming, friendly, and a good deal. The gracious owner and friendly staff at **La Boheme (42)** *(€-€€)* *(Via del Moro 2, 0583-462.404, www.boheme.it)* enhance the charm and elegance of this B&B; its spacious rooms and sumptuous breakfast add to its appeal.

MONTECATINI TERME (B)

With its plethora of hot springs, Tuscany has been a center for spas since ancient Roman times. In the early 20th century, Europe's aristocrats and royalty frequented the fashionable Montecatini Terme 0572-7781, *(www.termemontecatini.it)*, the elegant spa town. Each spa is notable for its architecture, and the formal gardens of the area add to the distinction of the town. **Terme Tettuccio**, grandly Neoclassical, has marble pools and Art Nouveau tiles; **Terme Torretta** holds teatime concerts; **Terme Leopoldine** resembles a classical temple; and **Terme Tamerici** offers splendid gardens.

Tourist Info: *(Viale Verdi 66/68, 0572-772.244, www. montecatini-terme.it)*

PLACES TO EAT & DRINK
Where to Eat:
Il Cucco (€€€) *(Via del Salsero 3, 0572-727.65; call for hours, closed Sa & Tu)* serves creative, delicious cuisine. For pastries or ice cream, try **Bargilli (€)** *(Viale Grocco 2, 0572-794.59, www.cialdedimontecatini.it; hours: Tu–Su 9AM–1PM, 3PM–8PM)*, known for *cialde* (almond cakes) and *brigidini* (waffle cookies).

Bars & Nightlife:
The disco **Le Panteraie** *(Via delle Panteraie 26, 0572-719.58, www.lepanteraie.it; call for hours)* does themed evenings and has a large outdoor pool.

NEARBY PLACES TO EAT & DRINK

Montecatini Alto: La Torre (€€€) *(Piazza Giusti 8/9, 0572-706.50, www.latorre-montecatinialto.it; call for hours, closed Tu)* is a friendly place for a home-cooked meal. Founded in 1878, **Caffè Kosì (€-€€)** *(Piazza Giusti 1, 0572-741.81, call for hours)* is a popular café and hangout.

WHERE TO STAY

Opulently Art Nouveau, Grand Hotel & La Pace (€€€-€€€€) *(Via della Torretta 1, 0572-9240, www.grand hotellapace.com)* offers luxurious rooms, a gorgeous garden, and a heated pool. Family-run Hotel Savoia & Campana (€) *(Viale Cavallotti 10, 0572-772.670, www. hotelsavoiaecampana.com)* is pleasant, comfortable, and spacious. La Pia (€) *(Via Montebello 30, 0572-786.00, www.lapiahotel.it)* is quiet, with simple, clean rooms.

NEARBY PLACES TO STAY

Montecatini Alto: Rustic yet sophisticated, Casa Albertina (€-€€) *(Via Fratelli Guermani 12, 0572-912.639 or 0572-910.172)* has simple furnishings and superb views.

PISTOIA (C)

Quiet, medieval-walled Pistoia was once a violent 13th-century town, thanks to two feuding groups, the Neri and the Bianchi (Blacks and Whites). They killed each other with locally made *pistole*, or small, thin daggers. Today Pistoia has traded daggers for  dogwood—its major activity is horticulture. The lovely historic center remains unmarred by tourism.

Tourist Info: APT *(Palazzo dei Vescovi, Piazza Duomo 4, 0573-216.22, www.pistoia.turismo.toscana.it)*

PLACES TO SEE
Landmarks, Arts & Entertainment:
Pistoia's Duomo, the **Cattedrale di San Zeno** *(Piazza del Duomo, 0573-250.95; hours: 8:30AM–12:30PM, 3:30PM–7PM)*, is strikingly zebra striped; its enameled terra-cotta doorway was made by Andrea della Robbia. In the **Cappella di San Jacobo** the amazing silver altar has over 600 statues and reliefs. Besides religious objects, the **Museo di San Zeno** *(Palazzo dei Vescovi, Piazza del Duomo, 0573-369.277; hours: Tu, Th–F 10AM–1PM, 3PM–5PM)* also displays Roman excavations in the basement. From medieval paintings to 20th-century artists and architects, the **Museo Civico** *(Palazzo del Comune, Piazza del Duomo 1, 0573-*

371.296; hours: winter Tu, Th–Sa 10AM–5PM, W 3PM–6PM, Su 11AM–5PM; summer Tu, Th–Sa 10AM–6PM, W 4PM–7PM, Su 11AM–6PM) spotlights the town's artists. **Centro Marino Marini** (Palazzo del Tau, Corso Silvano Fedi 30, 0573-302.85, www.fondazionemarinomarini.it; hours: M–Sa 10AM–6PM/5PM in winter) is dedicated to Pistoia's famous 20th-century artist Marini, with his bronze and clay sculptures, horse and rider pieces, and sculptures of Pomona, the ancient Roman fruit and fertility goddess.

NEARBY PLACES TO SEE

The lovely hillside village of **COLLODI**, favored by Carlo Collodi, author of *The Adventures of Pinocchio*, is home to **Pinocchio Park** (Via S. Gennaro 3, 0572-429.342, www.pinocchio.it; hours: 8:30AM–sunset) and the Baroque gardens of **Garzoni Gardens** (Piazza della Vittoria 1, 0572-427.314, www.pinocchio.it; hours: 8:30AM–sunset).

PLACES TO EAT & DRINK

Lo Storno (€-€€) (Via del Lastrone 8, 0573-261.93; hours: M–Sa 12PM–3PM, 7:30PM–10:30PM), founded in 1395, is a friendly trattoria with reliable food. The lovely **La Bottegaia** (€€) (Via del Lastrone 17, 0573-365.602, www.labottegaia.it; hours: Tu–Sa 10:30AM–3PM, 6:30PM–1AM, Su 6:30PM–1AM) has great food and plenty of charm. Laid-back **Trattoria dell'Abbondanza** (€€) (Via dell'Abbondanza 10/14, 0573-368.037; closed

Th lunch & W) serves traditional Tuscan food. **Gelateria di Paluzzi Maria Grazia & C. (€)** *(Via Cavour 53, 0573-227.58; hours: Tu–Sa 3:30PM–10PM)* is tiny, but its ices are grand.

WHERE TO SHOP

Riccio, cookies in the shape of hedgehogs, were the staples of feast days. **Bruno Corsini** *(Piazza San Francesco 42, 0573-201.38, www.brunocorsini.com; call for hours)* still makes them, along with other yummy sweets. For great Tuscan bread and *cantucci*, go to **Panetteria Capecchi** *(Viale Adua 175, 0573-277.75; call for hours)*.

WHERE TO STAY

Welcoming **Tenuta di Pieve a Celle** *(€€) (Via di Pieve a Celle 158, 0573-913.087, www.tenutadipieveacelle.it)*, a lovely *agriturismo* amid olive groves, cypresses, and vineyards, has wrought-iron beds, tile floors, and oriental rugs. **Hotel Firenze** *(€) (Via Curtatone e Montanara 42, 0573-231.41, www.hotel-firenze.it)* is friendly, simple, and comfortable.

PRATO (D)

A textile center since the 13th century, Prato attracts international designers for its high-quality fabrics, including recycled wools. The quiet suburb of Florence has recently been growing to expand its restaurants, bars, and tourist attractions. Prato was home to Francesco di Marco Datini, the 14th-century financial wizard who invented the promissory note and was the father of modern accounting. Datini was the inspiration for Iris Origo's 1957 novel *The Merchant of Prato*. The town is also a destination for tourists who come to see the Virgin's Girdle, a Christian relic housed in the Duomo, as well as the frescoes of Agnolo Gaddi and Filippo Lippi on display in the Duomo.

Tourist Info: APT *(Piazza Duomo 8, 0574-241.12, www.prato.turismo.toscana.it; hours: Oct–Mar M–F 9AM–1:30PM, 2:30PM–6:30PM, Sa 9AM–1:30PM, 2:30PM–6PM, Su 10AM–1PM; Apr–Sep M–Sa 9AM–1:30PM, 2:30PM–7PM, Su 10AM–1PM)*

PLACES TO SEE
Landmarks, Arts & Entertainment:

The façade of the Romanesque-Gothic **Duomo** *(Piazza del Duomo, 0574-262.34, call for hours)*, with green and white marble stripes, is unfinished. In the right corner stands the **Pulpit of the Holy Girdle**, designed by Michelozzo with a Dontello frieze of dancing children. Inside, the Virgin's Girdle *(Sacro Cingolo)*, the relic, is housed in the first chapel on the left. Agnolo Gaddi's frescoes tell the story: The Virgin Mary gave the belt to the Apostle Thomas, who passed it on to a Palestinian woman, who married a Pratese merchant in 1141 and brought the belt to Prato. The other highlight is Fra Filippo Lippi's *The Life of John the Baptist.* The **Museo dell'Opera del Duomo** *(Piazza del Duomo 49, 0574-293.39, www.cultura.prato.it/musei; hours: M, W–Sa 10AM–1PM, 3PM–6:30PM, Su 10AM–1PM)* contains Donatello's original panels from the Pulpit of the Holy Girdle, the beautiful carved gold coffer made to hold the Girdle, and Filippino Lippi's painting *St. Lucy.*

The **Museo di Pittura Murale** *(Piazza San Domenico 8, 0574-440.501; hours: Su–M, W–Th 9AM–1PM, F–Sa 9AM–1PM, 3PM–6PM)* houses Fra Filippo Lippi's *Madonna del Ceppo,* among other notable pieces. Baroque art is the focus of **Galleria degli Alberti** *(Palazzo Alberti, Via degli Alberti 2, 0574-617.359, www.galleriapallazzoalberti.it; hours: by appt),* with works by Lippi, Bellini, and Caravaggio.

Castello dell'Imperatore *(Piazza delle Carceri 0574-382.07; hours: Apr–Sep, W–M 9AM–1PM, 4PM–7PM; Oct–Mar, W–M 9AM–1PM),* built by German Holy Roman Emperor Frederick II, is an imposing 13th-century fortress. The **Museo del Tessuto** *(Via Santa Chiara 24, 0574-611.503, www.museodeltessuto.it; hours: M, W–F 10AM–6PM, Sa 10AM–2PM, Su 4PM–7PM)* has a fine textile collection; pieces range from early Christian times to today. Exhibits of contemporary art, conferences, classes, and concerts take place at the **Centro per l'Arte Contemporanea Luigi Pecci** *(Viale della Repubblica 277, 0574-5317, www.centropecci.it; call for hours)*. It also has a library, bookshop, and café.

NEARBY PLACES TO SEE

Poggio a Caiano: Villa Poggio a Caiano *(Piazza dé Medici 14, 055-877.012; hours: 8:15AM–4:30PM/7:30PM Jun–Aug)*, one of the grandest Medici villas, became a model for Renaissance villas to come; designed by Giuliano da Sangallo for Lorenzo the Magnificent, it is known for its beautiful frescoes.

PLACES TO EAT & DRINK

Local favorites for authentic, hearty Tuscan food are **Vecchia Cucina di Soldano** (€€) *(Via Pomeria 23, 0574-346.65; call for hours, closed Su)* and **Osteria Cibbe** (€-€€) *(Piazza Mercatale 49, 0574-607.509; call for hours, closed Su)*. The amazing desserts at elegant **Pasticceria Luca Mannori** (€) *(Via Lazzerini 2, at Via Pomeria, 0574-216.28, www.mannoriespace.it; call for hours)* make this genius pastry chef famous.

WHERE TO SHOP

In 1858, **Antonio Mattei** *(Via Ricasoli 20, 0574-257.56, www.antoniomattei.it; hours: Tu–F 8AM–7:30PM, Sa 8AM–1PM, 3:30PM–7:30PM, Su 8AM–1PM, closed July & 3 wks Aug)* invented *cantucci*; the bakery still sells these and other divine cookies.

WHERE TO STAY

Hotel Flora (€-€€) *(Via Cairoli 31, 0574-335.21, www.*

*hotelflora.info) offers large, well-designed rooms with modern amenities. A 16th-century country home, Villa Rucellai (€) (Via di Canneto 16, 0574-460.392, www.villarucellai.it) has a classical garden, vaulted ceilings, and quaint rooms. Hotel San Marco (€) (Piazza San Marco 48, 0574-213.21, www.hotelsanmarcoprato.com) is generically modern and comfortable.

NEARBY TOWNS

CARMIGNANO

Tourist Info: APT *(Piazza Vittorio Emanuele II 1-2, 055-871.2468; hours: summer Tu–Su 9AM–12:30PM, 3:30PM–7PM, winter Tu–F, 1st Su of month 9AM–12PM, 3:30PM–5:30PM, Sa–Su 9AM–12PM)*

PLACES TO SEE
Landmarks, Arts & Entertainment:

One of the oldest wine regions in the world, Carmignano vineyards include: **Tenuta di Capezzana** *(Via Capezzana 100, Seano, 055-870.6005, www.capezzana.it; call for tastings and tours)* and **Fattoria di Bacchereto** *(Via Fontemorana 179, 055-871.7191; hours: M–Sa 8AM–12:30PM, 2:30PM–6:30PM; tours/tastings by appt)*. Don't miss the **Church of San Michele** *(Piazza SS. Francesco e Michele, 055-871.2046; hours: Oct–Apr 7:30AM–5PM, May–Sep 7:30AM–6PM)*: it contains Pontormo's 1530 masterpiece *The Visitation.*

PLACES TO EAT & DRINK
Il Barco Reale *(€-€€) (Piazza Vittorio Emanuele II 26/28, 055-871.1559; call for hours, closed Tu)* serves typical Tuscan dishes, like *stracotto* (beef stewed in wine).

ARTIMINO

Tourist Info: See Prato office *(page 120)*.

PLACES TO SEE
Landmarks, Arts & Entertainment:

The many chimneys on Ferdinand I's hunting lodge **Villa La Ferdinanda** *(tours by appt, 055-875.1427)*, a notable Medici villa, have lent the place its nickname "Villa of a Hundred Chimneys." In the basement, the **Museo Archeologico** *(Via Papa Giovanni XXIII 5, 055-871.8124; hours: M–Tu, Th–Sa 9AM–12:30PM, Su 10AM–12PM; Nov–Jan Su 10AM–12PM)* is devoted to Etruscan and Roman artifacts from local excavations.

PLACES TO EAT & DRINK

One of Tuscany's best restaurants, **Da Delfina (€€-€€€)** *(Via della Chiesa 1, 055-871.8074, www.dadelfina.it; hours: Tu–Sa 12:30PM–2:30PM, 7:45PM–10:30PM, Su 12:30PM–2:30PM, closed Aug, cash only)* serves extraordinary seasonal Tuscan dishes on a fabulous terrace with a gorgeous view.

VINCI

Tourist Info: *(Via della Torre 11, 0571-568.012, www.comune.vinci.fi.it; hours: Mar–Oct 10AM–7PM, Nov–Feb M–F 10AM–3PM, Sa–Su 10AM–6PM)*

PLACES TO SEE
Landmarks, Arts & Entertainment:

The village of **Vinci** was Leonardo da Vinci's birthplace. The fantastic **Museo Leonardiano** *(Castello dei Conti Guidi, 0571-933.251, www.museoleonardiano.it; hours:*

Mar–Oct 9:30AM–7PM; Nov–Feb 9:30AM–6PM) contains the machines and instruments concocted by the genius. His home, **Casa di Leonardo** *(1 mile north, Anchiano, 0571-565.19, www.museoleonardiano.it/anchiano.htm; hours: Mar–Oct 9:30AM–7PM; Nov–Feb 9:30AM–6PM)*, is a simple farmhouse containing a few reproductions of his drawings.

PLACES TO EAT & DRINK
Il Ristoro del Museo (€€) *(Via Montalbano 9, 0571-565.16; call for hours, closed F dinner & Sa lunch)* has a view to die for and excellent food.

CARRARA (E)

The mountain quarries of Carrara have been producing their famous white marble since Roman times. They are

the oldest continuously operating industrial site in the world. Most of Imperial Rome was built of Carrara marble, and Michelangelo considered it the finest in the world: its light-reflecting properties make it seem translucent. Carrara is dedicated to the crafts involved in working the marble.

It is fitting that the film *The Agony and the Ecstasy*, with Charlton Heston as Michelangelo painting the Sistine Chapel, was shot here.

Tourist Info: *(Piazza Cesare Battisti 1, 0585-641.422, www.comune.carrara.ms.it; hours: M–T, Th, Sa 8:30AM–12:30PM)*

PLACES TO SEE
Landmarks, Arts & Entertainment:

Workshops in town offer the chance to see artisans at work crafting and sculpting marble. The **Museo Civico del Marmo** *(Viale XX Settembre, 0585-845.746, http://urano.isti.cnr.it:8880/museo/home.php; hours: May–Sep M–Sa 9:30AM–1PM, 3:30PM–6PM; Oct–Apr M–Sa 9AM–12:30PM, 2:30PM–5PM)* covers the techniques in detail. See lovely marble ornamentation at the **Duomo** *(Piazza del Duomo; open daily)*, also noted for the rose window in the façade, made from a single block of marble. On the square is the house, marked by a plaque, where Michelangelo stayed when marble shopping.

PLACES TO EAT & DRINK

For a cheap bite, **Pizzeria Tognozzi** (€) *(Via Santa Maria 12, 0585-717.50; call for hours, closed Su)* is quick and good. Toward the quarries, **Locanda Apuana** (€€) *(Via Comunale 1, 0585-768.017, www.locandaapuana.com; call for hours, closed Su dinner & M)* has great *tordelli*, meat and veggie ravioli. **Marina di Carrara: Ciccio Marina** (€€-€€€) *(Viale da Verrazzano 1, 0585-780.286; call for hours, Oct–May closed M)* serves seafood.

WHERE TO STAY

The 1960s Fosdinovo B&B (€) *(Via Montecarboli 12, Fosdinovo, 0187-684.65, www.fosdinovo-bb.com)* is a lovely, rustic country place in the rugged hills with a terrace, beautiful views, and an open-plan common area with fireplace.

VIAREGGIO & VERSILIA RIVIERA (F)

With its sandy beaches along the Gulf of Genoa and the magnificent Apuan Alps in the background, the Versilia Riviera became a resort area in the 19th century and remains a popular vacation spot. The privately run beaches charge entrance fees. Viareggio, surrounded by pine trees, is the main and most popular of the resort towns. Art Deco villas and cafés create a special allure reminiscent of the 1920s belied by the clubs along the coast. The town is famous for its carnival, the largest in Italy outside Venice. Increasingly gay and gay-friendly, the Versilia has a thriving GLBT scene.

Tourist Info: APT *(Viale Carducci 10, Viareggio, 0584-962.233, www.aptversilia.it, www.aboutversilia.com; call for hours)*

PLACES TO SEE
Landmarks, Arts & Entertainment:
Lido di Camaiore *(north of Viareggio)*, whose beach and boardwalk abut those of **Viareggio**, is family-oriented. Moving northward, the flora becomes more lush and the hotels less congested. Italian jet-setters favor the chic resort town **Forte dei Marmi** *(north of Marina di Pietrasanta)*, with its colorful seaside cabanas and picturesque 15th-century marble port. Villas of wealthy Italians

are nestled among the pines. **Marina di Pietrasanta** *(north of Lido di Camaiore)* offers trails through woods ideal for walking or biking. The nightlife in both is lively.

South of **Viareggio** is **Torre del Lago Puccini** *(Tourist Info: Viale Kennedy 2, 0584-359.893; call for hours)*, where the composer Giacomo Puccini summered. He is buried in **Museo Villa Puccini** *(Viale Puccini 266, 0584-341.445, www.giacomopuccini.it; hours: Apr–Oct Tu–Su 10AM– 12:40PM, 3PM–6:20PM, M 3PM–6:20PM; Nov–Jan Tu–Su 10AM–12:40PM, 2:30PM–5:10PM, M 2:30PM–5:10PM; Feb–Mar Tu–Su 10AM–12:40PM, 2:30PM–5:50PM, M 2:30PM–5:50PM)*, where his piano and gun rooms can be visited.

PLACES TO EAT & DRINK
Where to Eat:
Viareggio: The freshest seafood is in demand at hugely popular **Al Porto** *(€€-€€€)* *(Via Coppino 118, 0584- 383.878, www.alporto.it; call for hours, winter closed M, summer closed Su)*. Elegant **L'Oca Bianca** *(€€€)* *(Via Coppino 409, 0584-388.477, www.oca-bianca.it; open from 8PM)*, with a lovely view of the port, is a top-notch seafood restaurant. **Torre del Lago Puccini:** Elegant **Lombardi** *(€€)* *(Via Aurelia 127, 0584- 341.044; call for hours, closed Tu)* serves fine seafood dishes. Among the delicacies at **Da Cecco** *(€€)* *(Belvedere Puccini, 0584-341.022; call for hours, closed Su dinner & M)* are eel and frogs' legs. **Forte dei Marmi:** Classic, elegant, **Lorenzo** *(€€€€)* *(Via Carducci*

61, 0584-896.71; call for hours) invents inspired dishes, like turbot filet in aromatic herbs with zucchini and truffle flan. **Pietrasanta: Osteria alla Giudea (€-€€)** *(Via Barsanti 4, 0584-715.14; call for hours)* offers Tuscan dishes in a pleasant bistro space. **Camaiore:** Family-owned **Il Centro Storico (€€)** *(Via Cesare Battisti 66, 0584-989.786; call for hours, closed M)* serves simple dishes based on truffles and mushrooms as well as local classics.

Bars & Nightlife:

The seafront from Viareggio to Forte dei Marmi is lined with clubs; here are a few suggestions: **Viareggio: Voice Music Bar** *(Viale Margherita 63, 0584-943.321, www.galleriadeldisco.com; call for hours)* attracts a mixed gay/straight crowd. **Forte dei Marmi: La Capannina** *(Viale della Repubblica 18, 0584-801.69, www.lacapanninadifranceschi.it/cgi-bin/viewevento.cgi; hours: F–Sa 5:30PM–5AM)* is Versilia's oldest club, with music hall and ballroom dancing evenings. **Marina di Pietrasanta:** A young, trendy clientele fills **Twiga** *(Viale Roma 2, 0584-215.18, www.twigabeachclub.com; call for hours)*. **Seven Apples** *(Viale Roma 108, 0584-204.58, www.sevenapples.it; call for hours)* is hip, with a beachside bar, pool, and two dance floors. **Torre del Lago: Frau Marlene** *(Viale Europa, 0584-342.282; hours: F–Su 10PM–4AM)* is a trendy gay/lesbian club. A pub/Internet café/music club, **Priscilla Caffè** *(Viale Europa, 0584-341.804, www.priscillacaffe.it; call for hours)* regularly puts on drag queen shows.

WHERE TO STAY

Viareggio: Hotel Garden (€€) *(Via U. Foscolo 70, 0584-440.25, www.hotelgardenviareggio.it)* offers tasteful simplicity. Elegance envelops Hotel Plaza e de Russie (€-€€€) *(Piazza d'Azeglio 1, 0584-444.49, www.plazaederussie. com)*, a luxury hotel with a roof garden. Hotel Arcangelo (€) *(Via Carrara 23, 0584-471.23, www.hotelarcangelo. com)* is clean, quiet, and comfortable, with a lovely patio. **Lido di Camaiore:** Hotel Sylvia (€) *(Via Manfredi 15, 0584-617.994, www.hotelsylvia.it)*, a quiet, family-run hotel, has a lovely garden and airy rooms. **Camaiore:** Surrounded by steep hills, bougainvillea, jasmine, and lemon trees, Peralta (€-€€) *(Via Pieve 321, 0584-951.230, www.peraltatuscany.com)* is a quirky, rustic, friendly spread owned by a sculptress; art, writing, and cooking classes are offered. **Pietrasanta:** Subdued luxury and elegant simplicity infuse Albergo Pietrasanta (€€€-€€€€) *(Via Garibaldi 35, 0584-793.726, www.albergo pietrasanta.com)* with sophistication befitting the former home of a prestigious family.

Places to See:

1. Campo dei Miracoli
2. Leaning Tower
3. Duomo
4. Baptistery
5. Camposanto
6. Museo delle Sinopie
7. Museo dell'Opera del Duomo
8. Piazza dei Cavalieri
9. Museo Nazionale di San Matteo
10. Museo Nazionale di Palazzo Reale
11. Santa Maria della Spina
12. Solferino Bridge
13. San Paolo a Ripa d'Arno
14. Teatro Verdi

Places to Eat & Drink:

15. Al Ristoro dei Vecchi Macelli
16. Osteria dei Cavalieri
17. De Coltelli
18. Caffè dell'Ussero
19. Borderline
20. Cagliostro
21. Big Ben Pub

Where to Shop:

22. Corso Italia
23. Borgo Stretto
24. Mercatino Antiquario
25. De Bondt
26. Arturo Pasquinucci

Where to Stay:

27. Hotel Amalfitana
28. Hotel Repubblica Marinara
29. Relais dell'Orologio
30. Royal Victoria Hotel

V. Contessa Matilde

V. Card. Pietro Maffi

Pza. del
Duomo

Pza. Arcivescovado

Pza. Sta.
Caterina

Pza. Mattiri
d'Liberta

S. Stefano
d. Cavalieri

Pal. d.
Cavalieri

V. Santa Maria

V. dei
Mille

Pza. dei
Cavalieri

Orto
Botanico

Domus
Galilaeana

Pza. Dante
Alighieri

V. P. Savi

V. Roma

Pza.
Carrara

V. Risorgimento

V. Enrico Fermi

Pza.
Solferino

V. Voltturno

Ponte Pza.
Solferino Saffi

Lung. R. Simonelli

Lung-Sonnino

V. Francesco Crispi

Pza. di
Tersanaia

Ponte D.
Cittadella

Pza. S. Paolo
a Ripa d'Arno

V. C. Fazio

V. F. Niosi

V. Nino Bixio

V. Cesare Battisti

Lungarno Pacinotti

Gambacorti

V. Mazzini

Corso Italia

Pza. Vittotio
Emanuelle II

Pza.
Stazione

V. D'Argile

V. Gambsi

V. Filippo
Buonarotti

V. S. Zeno

Pza. S.
Francesco

V. San Lorenzo

V. Fuicini

V. Oberdan

V. Carducci

Pza. S. Paolo
all'Orta

Borgo Stretto

V. Fredriano

Pza.
Garibaldi

Pte. di
Mezzo

Pza. XX
Settembre

Pza. S.
Sepolcro

San Martino

V. Vicenzo S.

V. di Simone

V. Sigheri

Pza. d.
Gondole

Pza.
Repubblica

V. Cavour

Lungarno Medicco

Lung. Galileo Galilei

V. G. Bovio

V. G. Bruno

Pza.
Toniolo

V. Benedetto Croce

V. F. Bonaini

V. Amerigo Vespucci

V. F. Cortidoni

Pza.
Guerrazzi

Via A. Fratti

0   0.25 mile

0   0.25 km

A Ghibelline stronghold during the Middle Ages with a powerful naval fleet and trade presence, Pisa went into decline by the late 14th century and was taken over by Florence's Medicis. Today it has the aura of a minor city with a magnificent past. Known for the Campo dei Miracoli, including the Leaning Tower, and as Galileo's birthplace, Pisa offers many glorious sights.

Tourist Info: APT *(Piazza Duomo, 050-560.464; hours: M–Sa 9AM–6PM, Su 10:30AM–4:30PM; Piazza Vittorio Emanuele II 16, 050-422.91; hours: M–Sa 9AM–7PM, Su 9:30AM–3:30PM; Galilei Airport, 050-503.700; hours: 10:30AM–4:30PM, 6PM–10PM; www.comune.pisa.it/turismo)*

PLACES TO SEE
Landmarks, Arts & Entertainment:
Campo dei Miracoli (1) *(Piazza dei Miracoli, 050-835.011/12, www.opapisa.it)*, "Field of Miracles," is a fantastic complex of fabulous Romanesque buildings comprising some of the most important Pisan sights. They are a glorious mix of Romanesque colonnades,

Moorish marble inlays in geometric patterns, and Gothic spires and niches. At one end, the **Leaning Tower (2)** *(30 visitors every half hour; 050-835.011/12; hours: Dec–Jan 10AM–4:30PM, Nov, Feb 9:30AM–5:30PM, Mar 9AM–5:30PM, Apr, May, Sep 8:30AM–8PM, June–Aug 8:30AM–11PM, Oct 9AM–7PM)* is a belfry eight stories high with galleries of marble arcades circling six floors.

The tilt occurs because of the sandy subsoil and shallow foundations. The white marble **Duomo (3)** *(050-835.011/12; hours: Nov–Feb 10AM–12:45PM, 2PM–5PM, Mar 10AM–6PM, Apr–Sep 10AM–8PM, Oct 10AM–7PM)* has a façade of Moorish mosaics, inlays, and glass, with the cathedral architect Buscheto's wall tomb on the left. Touching the lizard in the brass doors is said to bring good luck. The **Baptistery (4)** *(050-835.011/12; hours: Nov–Feb 10AM–5PM, Mar 9AM–6PM, Apr–Sep 8AM–8PM, Oct 9AM–7PM)* is round with an onion-shaped dome. It houses a stupendous marble pulpit, by Nicola Pisano, carved with scenes from the life of Christ. The **Camposanto (5)** (Holy Field) *(050-835.011/12; hours: Nov–Feb 10AM–5PM, Mar 9AM–6PM, Apr–Sep 8:30AM–8PM, Oct 9AM–7PM)* is a field edged by an elaborate Romanesque-Gothic cemetery embellished by frescoes, such as Benozzo Gozzoli's *The Triumph of Death, Last Judgment,* and *Hell.* In World War II, the Allies bombed Camposanto, destroying frescoes; but the underlying sketches survived. They are housed in **Museo delle Sinopie (6)** *(050-835.011/12; hours: Nov–Feb 10AM–5PM, Mar 9AM–6PM, Apr–Sep 8AM–8PM, Oct 9AM–7PM)*, where you can also learn about the process of creating frescoes. The **Museo dell'Opera del Duomo (7)** *(050-835.011/12; hours: Nov–Feb 10AM–5PM, Mar 9AM–6PM, Apr–Sep 8AM–8PM, Oct 9AM–7PM)* contains artworks from the Duomo and Baptistery. It also houses 13th-century sculptures, such as Giovanni Pisano's ivory *Virgin and Child,* 15th- to 18th-century paintings, and Etruscan and Roman artifacts.

The beautiful **Piazza dei Cavalieri (8)**, mostly Giorgio Vasari's 16th-century designs, is the site of the prestigious university Scuola Normale Superiore, founded by Napoleon. Housed in a medieval convent, the **Museo Nazionale di San Matteo (9)** *(Piazzetta San Matteo in Soarta, 050-541.865; www.sbappsae-pi.beniculturali.it; hours: Tu–Su 8:30AM–7PM, holidays 9AM–1:30PM)* has an impressive collection of 12th- to 17th-century Pisan and Florentine art, including works by Simone Martini, Nino Pisano, Masaccio, Donatello, Fra Angelico, and Ghirlandaio. In a converted Medici palace, the **Museo Nazionale di Palazzo Reale (10)** *(Lungarno Pacinotti 46, 050-926.511 or 050-926.539, www.sbappsae-pi. beniculturali.it; hours: M, W–F 9AM–2:30PM, Sa 9AM– 1:30PM)* has collected artworks owned by the Medicis.

The little gem **Santa Maria della Spina (11)** *(Lungarno Gambacorti, 055-321.5446; hours: Nov–Feb Tu–Su 10AM–2PM, every 2nd Su of month 10AM–7PM; Mar–Oct Tu–F 10AM–1:30PM, 2:30PM–6PM, Sa–Su 10AM–1:30PM, 2:30PM–7PM)*, spikes and spires jutting from its rooftop, gets its name from the relic it houses: a thorn *(spina)* from Christ's Crown of Thorns. The nearby **Solferino Bridge (12)** affords a great view of the church and river, with Monte Pisano as backdrop. **San Paolo a Ripa d'Arno (13)** *(Piazza San Paolo a Ripa d'Arno, 050-415.15; hours by appt)* has a beautiful black and white marble façade; behind the apse, the unusual octagonal **Cappella Sant'Agata** is made of brick with a conical roof. Music, theater, and dance are performed at **Teatro Verdi (14)** *(Via Palestro 40, 050-941.111, www.teatrodipisa.pi.it)*.

PLACES TO EAT & DRINK
Where to Eat:

Al Ristoro dei Vecchi Macelli (15) (€€-€€€) *(Via Volturno 49, 050-204.24; call for hours)* is thoroughly Tuscan: try stuffed rabbit in creamy truffle sauce, pork ravioli in broccoli sauce, or the meat or fish samplers. Friendly **Osteria dei Cavalieri (16)** (€-€€) *(Via San Frediano 16, 050-580.858, www.osteriacavalieri.pisa.it; hours: M–F 12:30PM–2PM, 7:45PM–10PM, Sa 7:45PM–10PM, closed Aug)* one of the city's best trattorias, serves traditional dishes with a twist: *tagliolini* with rabbit and asparagus, or spaghetti with mussels and clams. Ice cream parlor **De Coltelli (17)** (€) *(Lungarno Pacinotti 23, 050-541.611, www.decoltelli.com; hours: 12PM–12:30AM)* has traditional and unusual flavors to cool your palette. Founded in 1794, **Caffè dell'Ussero (18)** (€) *(Lungarno Pacinotti 27, 050-581.100, www.ussero.com, cash only)* is an atmospheric literary café overlooking the Arno.

Bars & Nightlife:

There are several clubs and lounges to choose from for a night out on the town. **Borderline (19)** *(Via Vernaccini 7, 050-580.577; call for hours)* offers live blues and country from time to time, in addition to hard rock, alternative, and reggae. A copper and metal interior at **Cagliostro (20)** *(Via del Castelletto 26-30, 050-575.413; hours: M–Sa 7:30PM–1AM)* sets the tone for this unusual yet relaxing place: it has a great menu, large wine list, and art exhibits. **Big Ben Pub (21)** *(Via Palestro 11, 050-581.158; hours: until 2AM)*, typically English, serves beer and pub food.

WHERE TO SHOP

The main shopping streets are **Corso Italia (22)** and **Borgo Stretto (23)**. The antiques market, **Mercatino Antiquario (24)** *(Largo Ciro Menotti, 2nd weekend of month, 050-910.111)*, also sells modern arts and crafts. **De Bondt (25)** *(Lungarno Pacinotti 5, 050-316.0073, www.debondt.it; call for hours)* is among the world's top *cioccolatieri* (chocolatiers). **Arturo Pasquinucci (26)** *(Via Oberdan 22, 050-580.140, www.pasquinucci.it; call for hours)* sells crystal, glass, ceramics, and kitchen goods.

WHERE TO STAY

Hotel Amalfitana (27) (€) *(Via Roma 44, 050-290.00, www.hotelamalfitana.it)*, a small family-run hotel, is in a 15th-century palazzo. On the outskirts of the town is **Hotel Repubblica Marinara (28)** (€€) *(Via Matteucci 81, 050-387.0100, www.hotelrepubblicamarinara.it)*, large, modern, efficient, and electronically equipped. Luxury boutique hotel **Relais dell'Orologio (29)** (€€€-€€€€) *(Via della Faggiola 12-14, behind Piazza dei Cavalieri, 050-830.361, www.hotelrelaisorologio.com)* is exceptional in every way: stenciled ceiling beams, elegant furnishings, and a sumptuous dining room. **Royal Victoria Hotel (30)** (€-€€) *(Lungarno Pacio Pacinotti 12, 050-940.111, www.royalvictoria.it)* is an upscale hotel with a medieval tower and spectacular views of the Arno and beyond.

SAN MINIATO (H)

The skyline of San Miniato, high on a hill, is a picturesque image punctuated by the fortress tower, the brick buttresses of San Francesco Monastery, and aristocratic 15th- to 17th-century palazzi. The town is known for great truffles and its annual National Kite Flying Championships which take place after Easter.

Tourist Info: Ufficio di Turismo *(Piazza del Popolo 1, 0571-427.45, www.cittadisanminiato.it; call for hours)*

PLACES TO SEE
Landmarks, Arts & Entertainment:
The red-brick façade of the **Duomo** *(Piazza del Duomo)* dates from the 12th century. Among artwork in the **Museo Diocesano d'Arte Sacra** *(Piazza del Duomo, 0571-418.071; call for hours)* is Filippo Lippi's *Crucifixion* and a terra-cotta bust of Christ thought to be by Verrocchio. **Piazza della Repubblica** is home to a 17th-century seminary decorated in frescoes and plaster etchings of the Virtues, as well as lovely restored 15th-century shops. There's a marvelous view of the town, the Pisan hills, and the Arno Valley from **Spiazzo del Castello**, the Esplanade of the **Rocca** *(behind the Museo Diocesano)*, Frederick II's castle.

PLACES TO EAT & DRINK
Enjoy the pasta and the spectacular view at **Caffè Centrale (€)** *(Via IV Novembre 19, 0571-430.37; call for hours, closed M)*. Vegetarian and traditional dishes are

the fare at **Il Convio** (€€) *(Via San Maiano 2, 0571-408.114, www.ristoranteilconvio.com; call for hours, closed W)*. Enjoy the ambience as you dine underneath the brick vaulted ceilings at the lovely **Ristorante Castelvecchio** (€€-€€€) *(Via Castelvecchio 11, 0571-484.033, www.villasonnino.com; call for hours)*, housed in the picturesque Villa Sonnio.

WHERE TO SHOP

Il Cantuccio di Federigo *(Via P. Maioli 67, 0571-418.344; call for hours)* produces marvelous biscuits: *cantucci*, sweet *panettone* bread, *brigidino* (crunchy thin wafer), or buttery *colomba*.

WHERE TO STAY

Overlooking the Arno Valley, Miravalle Palace Hotel (€) *(Piazza del Castello 3, 0571-418.075, www.albergo miravalle.com)* has simple furnishings in spacious rooms.

LIVORNO (I)

From a small fishing village in 1571, Livorno grew to become one of Italy's busiest ports. By the early 1600s it was open to all traders, regardless of race, nationality, or religion. It became a haven for those fleeing religious persecution, and Jews, Arabs, Turks, Protestants, and others made Livorno into a cosmopolitan success story.

Tourist Info: APT *(Piazza Cavour 6, 0586-204.611, www.costadeglietruschi.it; hours: M–F 9AM–1PM, 3PM–5PM, Sa 9AM–1PM)*

PLACES TO SEE
Landmarks, Arts & Entertainment:

The monument *I Quattro Mori (Piazza Micheli)* commemorates the defeat of the Moors by the Knights of St. Stephen. Its figure of Duke Ferdinand I on a pedestal was created in 1594; the four chained Moorish slaves were added in 1626. The heart of Livorno is around **Porto Mediceo** and the lovely **Venezia Nuova** district, with its canals, bridges, and narrow streets.

PLACES TO EAT & DRINK

Don't miss Livorno's famous spicy fish stew, *cacciucco*. Renown for its authentic Livornese dishes, **Da Galileo** (€-€€) *(Via della Campana 20, 0586-889.009, www.trattoria dagalileo.blogspot.com; call for hours, closed W, Su dinner)* is a cozy, old-fashioned fish restaurant. One of the best fish places is **La Chiave** (€€-€€€) *(Scali delle Cantine 52, 0586-829.865; hours: Th–Tu 12PM–3PM, 7:30PM–11PM)*. For your ice cream fix, head for **La Chiostra** (€) *(Viale Italia 8, 0586-813.564; call for hours)*.

WHERE TO STAY

Hotel Gran Duca (€€) *(Piazza Micheli 16, 0586-891.024, www.granduca.it)* is large, sophisticated, and fully tech-equipped.

chapter 5

SIENA AND CENTRAL TUSCANY

SIENA AND CENTRAL TUSCANY

A. SIENA ★
B. SAN GALGANO
C. SAN GIMIGNANO ★
D. VOLTERRA ★

E. CHIANTI REGION ★
F. MONTALCINO ★
G. PIENZA ★
H. MONTEPULCIANO ★

• SNAPSHOT •

One of the most picturesque regions of Italy is central Tuscany. Rolling hills, small hamlets, isolated farmhouses, vineyards, olive groves, and tall cypress trees are characteristic of the area. Between Florence and Siena lies the Chianti region, hilly, wooded, and renowned for some of the world's finest wines as well as olive oil and pecorino cheese. The Crete Senesi, or "Sienese clay hills," lie to the southeast of the region's main town, Siena. This area produces the pink brick so prevalent throughout Tuscany.

Central Tuscany is full of spectacular medieval walled towns, such as San Gimignano, Pienza, and Radda in Chianti. Breathtakingly beautiful hilltop towns, such as Montalcino, Montepulciano, and San Quirico d'Orcia are marvelous specimens of ancient cultures. While village streets are themselves living works of art, museums abound. Etruscan and Roman artifacts as well as medieval and Renaissance art are preserved in the Sistema Musei Senesi *(www.museisenesi.org)*, a regional museum network.

TOP PICK!

SIENA ★

Places to See:

1. Piazza del Campo
2. Fonte Gaia
3. Torre del Mangia
4. Palazzo Pubblico
5. Duomo
6. Museo dell'Opera del Metropolitana
7. Santa Maria della Scala
8. Pinacoteca Nazionale
9. Via della Galluzza
10. Santuario e Casa di Santa Caterina
11. Basilica di San Domenico
12. Piazza Salimbeni
13. Fortezza Medicea
14. Orto Botanico
15. Palazzo delle Papesse

Places to Eat & Drink:

16. Osteria Le Logge
17. Liberamente Osteria
18. Antica Trattoria Papei
19. Da Mugolone
20. Pasticceria Bini
21. Gelateria Brivido
22. Nannini
23. Caffè Fiorella
24. Enoteca Italiana
25. Enoteca I Terzi
26. Dublin Post

Where to Shop:

27. General Market
28. Antiques Market
29. Antichità Sena Vetus
30. Ceramiche Artistiche Santa Caterina
31. Siena Ricama
32. Antica Drogheria Manganelli
33. Enoteca San Domenico
34. Martini Marisa
35. Il Telaio
36. Book Shop

Where to Stay:

37. Hotel Antica Torre
38. Hotel Garden
39. Hotel Santa Caterina
40. Residence Paradiso
41. Grand Hotel Continental
42. Palazzo Ravizza

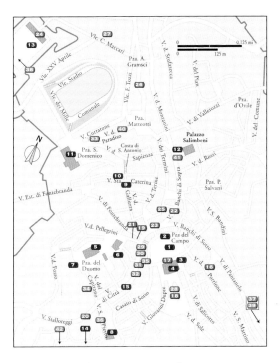

More than in most Italian cities,
to turn a corner in Siena is to
be presented with a gift.

—*Kate Simon*

Siena, Florence's age-old rival, is a glorious walled city of narrow streets, superb museums and churches, and beautiful, peaceful corners. Yellow-brown buildings on steep hills give it a mystical aura, as does its renown as the birthplace of Saint Catherine.

Tourist Info: APT *(Piazza del Campo 56, 0577-280. 551, www.terresiena.it or www.comune.siena.it; hours: 9AM–7PM)*

PLACES TO SEE
Landmarks, Arts & Entertainment:
Siena's central square, shell-shaped **Piazza del Campo (1)**, is one of Italy's most beautiful piazzas. Encircled by elegant buildings, it has nine sections, representing the "Council of Nine," the nine magistrates of the guilds. On one side of the piazza, the **Fonte Gaia (2)** (Fountain of Joy) by Jacopo della Quercia, is the end point of 16 miles of acqueducts. There is a story that when the fountain was being built an ancient statue of Venus was uncovered; when the plague hit Siena (1348–1350), the Sienese blamed Venus, shattered the statue, and buried the rubble in Florentine territory. Rising above the Campo, the bell tower **Torre del Mangia (3)** *(0577-292.614/5; hours: Mar–mid-Oct 10AM–7PM, mid-Oct–Feb 10AM–4PM)* affords wonderful views from the top. It was Italy's tallest tower when first built. The tower abuts **Palazzo Pubblico (4)**, the town hall, which houses the **Museo Civico** *(Palazzo Pubblico, Piazza del Campo, 0577-292.614/5, www.comune.siena.it; hours: mid-Mar–Oct 10AM–7PM; Nov–mid-Mar 10AM–6PM)*. It

contains 16th to 19th-century art as well as 14th-century works, most notably Simone Martini's 1315 fresco of the Virgin, the *Maestà*. If you're in Siena in either July or August, you won't want to miss Italy's most famous horse race, the

Palio di Siena *(Piazza del Campo, see page 27 for more details.)*

The **Duomo (5)** *(Piazza Duomo, 0577-283.048, www. operaduomo.siena.it; call for hours or visit Web site)* is a fabulous Gothic cathedral of black and white marble with a spectacular inlaid marble floor, Pinturicchio frescoes, and a carved pulpit by Pisano. Part of the unfinished nave was turned into the **Museo dell'Opera del Metropolitana (6)** *(Piazza Duomo 8, 0577-283.048, www.operaduomo.siena.it; hours: M–F 9AM–1PM)*, housing artwork from the cathedral. The **Santa Maria della Scala (7)** *(Piazza Duomo 7, 0577-534.511, www.santa mariadellascala.com; hours: 10:30AM–6:30PM)* museum complex covers the history of Siena through art, archaeology, and culture. **Pinacoteca Nazionale (8)** *(Via San Pietro 29, 0577-286.143; hours: Su–M 9AM–1PM, Tu–Sa 10AM–6PM)* is especially known for its important collection of Sienese masters.

Just northwest of the **Piazza del Campo (1)** is **Via della Galluzza (9)**, a lovely, steep medieval street. The **Santuario e Casa di Santa Caterina (10)** *(Costa di Sant'Antonio, 0577-*

247.393; hours: Easter–Oct 9AM–12:30PM, 3PM–6PM; winter 9AM–12:30PM, 3:30PM–6PM) is the birthplace and sanctuary of patron St. Catherine of Siena, who persuaded Pope Gregory XI to return the papacy to Rome from Avignon in 1376. When she died, heretics dismembered her, but her head is in a tabernacle in the **Basilica di San Domenico (11)** *(Piazza San Domenico, 0577-286.848, www.basilicacateriniana.com; hours: Mar–Oct 7AM–6:30PM, Nov–Feb 9AM–6PM)*.

On the spectacular **Piazza Salimbeni (12)** are three gorgeous palazzi, each in a different architectural style: Salimbeni, Spannocchi, and Tantucci. There are beautiful views of the city at **Fortezza Medicea (13)** *(Viale C. Maccari)*. Even more tranquil, the Botanical Garden, **Orto Botanico (14)** *(Via Mattioli 4, 0577-232.874; hours: M–F 8AM–5:30PM, Sa 8AM–12:30PM)*, brings the countryside into the city. **Palazzo delle Papesse (15)** *(Via di Città 126, 0577-220.71, www. papesse.org; hours: Tu–Su 11AM–7PM)* mounts contemporary art exhibits.

PLACES TO EAT & DRINK
Where to Eat:
Osteria Le Logge (16) (€€–€€€) *(Via del Porrione 33, 0577-480.13; hours: M–Sa 12PM–2:45PM, 7PM–10:30PM, closed Jan 1–Feb 7)* provides excellent traditional cuisine in a beautiful old palazzo. The same owners run **Liberamente Osteria (17)** (€–€€) *(Piazza del Campo 27, 0577-274.733, www.liberamenteosteria.it; hours: M–Sa 10AM–11:30PM)*, a fabulous wine bar with interiors designed by Sandro Chia and good eats. The family atmosphere at

Antica Trattoria Papei (18) (€–€€) *(Piazza del Mercato 6, 0577-280.894; hours: Tu–Su 12PM–3PM, 7PM–10:30PM)* is as authentic as the Sienese dishes and beamed ceilings. One of Siena's best restaurants, **Da Mugolone (19)** (€€€–€€€€) *(Via dei Pellegrini 8, 0577-283.235; hours: M–W, F–Sa 12:30PM–3PM, 7:30PM–10PM, Su 12:30PM–3PM)* is chic, simple, and does the best truffles and mushrooms. **Pasticceria Bini (20)** (€) *(Via di Stalloreggi 91, 0577-280.207; hours: Tu–Su 8AM–1PM, 4:15PM–8:15PM)* is a marvelous pastry shop; try the panforte or cannoli. For great ice cream, try **Gelateria Brivido (21)** (€) *(Via dei Pellegrini 1, 0577-280.058; call for hours, open Mar–Oct)*.

Outside Siena, the creative Mediterranean cuisine of **Antica Trattori Botteganova** (€€€–€€€€) *(Rte SS408, toward Chianti, Strada Chiantigiana 29, 0577-284.230; hours: 12:30PM–2:30PM, 7:30PM–10:30PM)* is delicious; the ambience, elegant.

Bars & Nightlife:

Piazza del Campo (1) is lined with lovely cafés, a great spot to rest and watch the crowds. Siena's most famous café, **Nannini (22)** *(Via Banchi di Sopra 22-24, 0577-236.009; hours: 7:30AM–12AM)* is great for drinks, coffee, or desserts. For the best coffee, go to **Caffè Fiorella (23)** *(Via di Città 13, 0577-271.255; hours: M–Sa 7AM–7:30PM)*. **Enoteca Italiana (24)** *(Fortezza Medicea, Piazza Libertà 1, 0577-228.832/43, www.enoteca-italiana.it; hours: M–Sa*

12PM–1AM) stocks a huge variety of wines; tastings are held daily. Amid medieval walls, **Enoteca I Terzi (25)** (*Via dei Termini 7, 0577-443.29, www.enotecaiterzi.it; hours: M–Sa 11AM–1AM*) offers good wines and snacks. From the music to the beer, the **Dublin Post (26)** (*Piazza Gramsci 20-21, 0577-289.089, www.dublinpost.it; hours: M–Sa 12PM–2AM, Su 6PM–2AM*) rocks.

WHERE TO SHOP

Siena's main shopping streets are **Via di Città** and **Via Banchi di Sopra**, elegant, narrow, serpentine cobbled passageways. At Siena's great **General Market (27)** (*La Lizza; hours: W 8AM–1PM*), vendors sell produce, flowers, crafts, shoes, and handbags. The **Antiques Market (28)** (*Piazza del Mercato*) is held every month on the third Sunday. **Antichità Sena Vetus (29)** (*Via di Città 53, 0577-423.95; call for hours*) deals in spectacular antique furniture and jewelry. Some of the pottery at **Ceramiche Artistiche Santa Caterina (30)** (*Via di Città 51 & 74-6, 0577-283.098; hours: 10AM–8PM*) is inspired by the Duomo's floor. The embroidery and needlepoint at **Siena Ricama (31)** (*Via di Città 61, 0577-288.339; hours: M–F 9:30AM–1PM, 2:30PM–7PM, Sa 9:30AM–1PM*) take motifs from medieval art. Founded in 1879, **Antica Drogheria Manganelli (32)** (*Via di Città 71-73, 0577-280.002; call for hours*) is a beautiful gourmet grocery store. **Enoteca San Domenico (33)** (*Via del Paradiso 56, 0577-271.181, www.enotecasandomenico.it; call for hours*) stocks wines from small to large producers, as well as other alcohol, olive oil, and their own cakes. **Martini Marisa (34)** (*Via del Capitano 5/11, at Piazza del Duomo,*

0577-226.438; hours: 9:30AM–8PM) carries gorgeous hand-painted *majolica*. **Il Telaio (35)** *(Chiasso del Bargello 2, 0577-470.65; hours: M–Sa 9:30AM–7:30PM)* sells handmade leather accessories and men's and women's clothing. The goods at **Book Shop (36)** *(Via di San Pietro 19, 0577-226.594, www.book shopsiena.com; hours: M–Sa 10AM–7:30PM)* are in English, with lots of wine books; the shop also hosts book launches.

WHERE TO STAY

In a restored 16th-century tower, **Hotel Antica Torre (37)** *(€-€€) (Via di Fiera Vecchia 7, 0577-222.255, www. anticatorresiena.it)* combines modern comfort with a sense of history. **Hotel Garden (38)** *(€€) (Via Custoza 2, 0577-567.111, www.gardenhotel.it)* has a garden and pool; rooms have great views. Antiques and a terraced garden add charm to **Hotel Santa Caterina (39)** *(€€) (Via Piccolomini 7, 0577-221.105, www.hscsiena.it)*. Small furnished apartments at **Residence Paradiso (40)** *(€) (Via del Paradiso 16, 0577-222.613, www.residenceparadiso. siena.it)* have kitchens and laundry rooms. Small but sumptuous, the exceptional **Grand Hotel Continental (41)** *(€€€€) (Via Banchi di Sopra 85, 0577-560.11, www. royaldemeure.com)* has opulent rooms, parlors, and ballrooms. Tastefully decorated with antiques, **Palazzo Ravizza (42)** *(€€-€€€) (Pian dei Mantellini 34, 0577-280.462, www.palazzoravizza.it)* has a lovely garden and the intimacy of a home.

SAN GALGANO (B)

Southwest of Siena, an air of mystery surrounds the abandoned Gothic abbey **Abbazia di San Galgano** *(Rte SP73; hours: 8AM–12PM, 2PM–sunset, www.sangalgano. org)*, rising out of the woods like a specter. The knight Galgano (1148–1181), devoting himself to God and rejecting violence and the material world, flung his sword at a boulder; it became embedded to the hilt, which he took as a sign from God. The sword in the stone is inside the door of the oratory.

Italy is a dream that keeps
returning for the rest
of your life.

–Anna Akhmatova

SAN GIMIGNANO ⭐

TOP PICK!

San Gimignano is a gorgeous, well-preserved medieval town on a hill with a distinctive skyline of soaring stone towers. Its beauty, however, is nearly lost in the sea of tourists in the summer during the day; however, it becomes magical at night.

Tourist Info: Pro Loco *(Piazza del Duomo 1, 0577-940.008, www.sangimignano.com or www.comune.san gimignano.si.it; hours: Mar–Oct 9AM–1PM, 3PM–7PM; Nov–Feb 9AM–1PM, 2PM–6PM)*

PLACES TO SEE
Landmarks, Arts & Entertainment:

There is a plethora of museums in San Gimignano while works of contemporary sculpture throughout the town contrast with its medieval architecture. The cathedral, the **Collegiata** *(Piazza del Duomo, 0577-940.316; call for hours)*, is full of fabulous frescoes, and the arches along the nave are stunningly striped blue and white. The **Museo Civico** *(Palazzo del Popolo, Piazza del Duomo, 0577-990.312; hours: Mar–Oct 9:30AM–7PM, Nov–Feb 10AM–5:30PM)* houses 14th- to 16th-century art. The **Torre Grossa**, in the same building, looks out on a breathtaking panorama of terra-cotta rooftops,

stone towers, and sloping hills. Art from the **Collegiata**, paintings, and sculpture form the collection of the **Museo d'Arte Sacra** *(Piazza Pecori, 0577-940.316; hours: Mar, Nov–Jan 20 M–Sa 9:30AM–4:40PM, Su 12:30–4:40PM; Apr–Oct M–F 9:30AM–7:10PM, Sa 9:30AM–5:10PM, Su 12:30PM–5:10PM)*. Don't miss the lovely stone well in **Piazza della Cisterna**. The **Rocca** *(Piazza Propositura)*—or "Fortress"—is part of a public garden with fig and olive trees; it offers lovely views.

PLACES TO EAT & DRINK
Where to Eat:
At **Ristorante Dorandò** (€€€) *(Vicolo dell'Oro 2, 0577-941.862, www.ristorantedorando.it; hours: Tu–Su 12PM–2:30PM, 7PM–9:30PM, also open M Easter–Nov)*, ancient recipes mesh with innovative modern cuisine. Try great old local dishes, like venison with pine nuts, raisins, chocolate, and vinegar, at **La Mangiatoia** (€-€€) *(Via Mainardi 5, 0577-941.528; hours: W–M 12:30PM–2:30PM, 7:30PM–10PM)*. Local favorite **La Mandragola** (€-€€) *(Via Berignano 58, 0577-940.377; call for hours)* serves traditional fare. Feast your eyes on the pastries and chocolates at **Pasticceria Armando e Marcella** (€) *(Via San Giovanni 88, 0577-941.051; call for hours)*. For ice cream, stop by **Gelateria di Piazza** (€) *(Piazza della Cisterna 4, 0577-942.244, www.gelateriadipiazza.com; call for hours)*.

Bars & Nightlife:
The popular **Avalon Pub** *(Viale Roma 1, 0577-940.023, www.avalon-pub.com; call for hours)* has live music, Internet stations, and a terrace. Another favorite bar,

Da Gustavo *(Via San Matteo 29, 0577-940.057; call for hours)* is always packed.

WHERE TO SHOP

Via San Giovanni is full of galleries, jewelers, wine sellers, stores specializing in wild boar products, and lots of tacky souvenir shops. **I Ninnoli** *(Via San Matteo 3, 0577-943.011, www.ininnolisangimignano.com; call for hours)* sells mostly handmade home decorations, specializing in Florentine-style lamps. Work of local artisans, from leather goods to pottery to masks, is the specialty of **Tinacci Tito & Maria Grazia** *(Via San Giovanni 41a, 0577-940.345 or 0577-940.054, www.tinacci.com; call for hours)*. **Azienda Agricola Il Casale-Falchini** *(Via di Casale 40, 0577-941.305, www.falchini.com; call for hours)* sells wines from its own estates.

WHERE TO STAY

Beautiful L'Antico Pozzo (€€) *(Via San Matteo 87, 0577-942.014, www.anticopozzo.com)* has retained the elegant character of the 15th-century residence where Dante once slept. In an atmospheric 12th-century palazzo, Leon Bianco (€-€€) *(Piazza della Cisterna, 0577-941.294, www.leonbianco.com)* offers lovely rooms with great views. Upscale Relais Santa Chiara (€€-€€€) *(Via Matteotti 15, 0577-940.701, www.rsc.it)* has spacious rooms, many with balconies, and a serene garden. Rafters, fireplaces, and lovely tiles give charm and grace to Fattoria Guicciardini (€€) *(Viale Garibaldi 2a, Piazza S. Agostino 1, 0577-907.185, www.guicciardini.com)*, a converted 15th-century farmhouse.

NEARBY PLACES TO STAY

Charming **Fortezza de' Cortesi** (€€) *(Monti area, 0577-940.123, www.fortezzacortesi.com, weekly rentals)* turns the stones, vaulted ceilings, and wood beams into defining touches of this lovely villa. Toward **Pancole** and **Certaldo** are several lovely B&Bs in serene surroundings with great views: **Il Casale del Cotone** (€-€€) *(Cellole area, 0577-943.236, www.casaledelcotone.com)*; **La Fonte** (€€) *(Via Canonica 4, 0577-944.845, www.la-fonte.com)*; **Il Rosolaccio** (€-€€) *(Capezzano area, 0577-944.465, www.rosolaccio.com)*; and **Agriturismo Podere Villuzza** (€-€€) *(Strada 25, 0577-940.585, www.poderevilluzza.it)*.

NEARBY TOWNS

CERTALDO
Tourist Info: *(Piazza Masini 2, 0571-656.721, www.prolococertaldo.it; hours: 9AM–1PM, 3:30PM–7PM, closed Jan–mid-Mar)*

PLACES TO SEE
Landmarks, Arts & Entertainment:
Certaldo is the hometown of Giovanni Boccaccio, author of *The Decameron*. **Museo-Casa del Boccaccio** *(Via Boccaccio 18, 0571-661.265 or 0571-664.208, www.casaboccaccio.it; hours: Apr–Oct 9:30AM–1:30PM, 2:30PM–7PM; Nov–Mar 9:30AM–1:30PM, 2:30PM–4:30PM)* is dedicated to his life and work.

PLACES TO EAT & DRINK
Osteria del Vicario (€€-€€€) *(Via Rivellino 3, 0571-*

668.228, www.osteriadelvicario.it; call for hours) is a great restaurant with imaginatively prepared dishes. **La Saletta di Dolci Follie** *(€€) (Via Roma 3, 0571-668.188; call for hours, closed Tu)* has good wines, standard fare, and pastries.

WHERE TO STAY
Fattoria del Bassetto *(€) (Via delle Città 3, 0571-668.342, www. fattoriabassetto.com)*, a working farm producing olive oil and honey, has rooms and dorms in a converted monastery; on weekends there are wine tastings and a bar with a band.

COLLE DI VAL D'ELSA
Tourist Info: *(Via Campana 43, 0577-922.791/621, www.comune.collevaldelsa.it; call for hours; also, Piazza Arnolfo di Cambio 9a, 0577-921.334; hours: M–Sa 6:40AM–8:10PM, Su 8AM–8:10PM)*

PLACES TO SEE
Landmarks, Arts & Entertainment:
The charming **Colle di Val d'Elsa** is known for crystal-making. See artisans at work in crystal workshops or check out the artistry at the **Museo del Cristallo** *(Via dei Fossi, 0577-924.135, www.cristallo.org; hours: Easter–Oct Tu–Su 10AM–12PM, 4PM–7:30PM; Nov–Easter Tu–F 3PM–7PM, Sa–Su 10AM–12PM, 3PM–7PM).*

PLACES TO EAT & DRINK

Excellent cuisine, refined service, and a 16th-century palazzo make **Arnolfo (€€€€)** *(Via XX Settembre 50, 0577-920.549, www.arnolfo.com; call for hours, closed Tu–W, Jan 22–Mar 4, & July 29–Aug 13)* one of Tuscany's top restaurants.

WHERE TO SHOP

The crystal-making tradition here dates from Etruscan times. **Belli** *(Via Diaz 23, 0577-926.749; call for hours)* produces fine crystal in the old style. **Sandra Mezzetti Cristallerie** *(Via Oberdan 13, 0577-920.395, www. cristalleriemezzetti.com; hours: M 3:30PM–8PM, Tu–Sa 9AM–1PM, 3:30PM–8PM)* sells crystal made by the finest craftsmen. Or shop at **La Grotta del Cristallo** *(Via del Muro Lungo 20, 0577-924.676, www.lagrottadel cristallo.it; call for hours)* for creative crystal designs.

VOLTERRA

TOP PICK!

An ancient Etruscan town, Volterra stands on a hill with lovely views of the surrounding slopes and valleys. It is known for the white alabaster statues carved by local artisans.

Tourist Info: Associazione Pro Volterra *(Piazza dei Priori 10, 0588-861.50, www.provolterra.it)*

Tourist Office: *(Piazza dei Priori 20, 0588-872.57, www. volterra-toscana.net)*

PLACES TO SEE
Landmarks, Arts & Entertainment:
The famous **Museo Etrusco Guarnacci** *(Via Don Minzoni 15, 0588-863.47; hours: mid-Mar–Oct 9AM–7PM, Nov–mid-Mar 9AM–2PM)* has one of the finest collections of Etruscan artifacts in the world; one of the highlights is a thin, long bronze statue called *Ombra della Sera,* "Evening Shadow." Part Etruscan, part Roman, the **Arco Etrusco** *(Via Porta all'Arco)* is a huge 4th-century B.C. stone arch in the town's Etruscan wall. The **Duomo** *(Piazza San Giovanni)* contains work by Mino da Fiesole, Guglielmo Pisano, Fra Bartolomeo, and Zaccaria da Volterra, among others. The **Museo d'Arte Sacra/Museo Opera del Duomo** *(Via Roma 13, 0588-862.90/0588-861.92; hours: mid-Mar–Oct 9AM–1PM, 3PM–6PM, Nov–mid-Mar 9AM–1PM)* houses sculpture, architectural fragments, and 11th- to 15th-century bells from various churches. Behind this museum and the

Duomo is the beautiful **Piazza dei Priori**, while marvelous palazzi line **Via dei Sarti**. Fine works by Florentine artists are collected in the **Pinacoteca** *(Palazzo Minucci-Solaini, Via dei Sarti 1, 0588-875.80; hours: mid-Mar–Oct 9AM–7PM, Nov–mid-Mar 9AM–1PM)*; highlights include Rosso Fiorentino's *The Deposition*, Ghirlandaio's *Christ in Majesty*, and Luca Signorelli's *Madonna and Child with Saints* and *Annunciation*. Dating from the 1st century B.C., **Teatro Romano** *(Porta Fiorentina, Viale Ferrucci, 0588-860.50; hours: mid-Mar–Oct 10:30AM–5:30PM, Nov–mid-Mar Sa–Su 10AM–4PM)* is well preserved and reconstructed. For fabulous views, stroll the **Viale dei Ponti**, south of the fortress.

PLACES TO EAT & DRINK
Where to Eat:
Trattoria del Sacco Fiorentino (€€) *(Piazza XX Settembre 18, 0588-885.37; call for hours, closed W)* is a good restaurant with delicious comfort food. Sophisticated **Del Duca** (€€) *(Via di Castello 2, 0588-815.10, www.enoteca-delduca-ristorante.it; call for hours, closed Tu)* has a lovely garden.

Bars & Nightlife:
The bar **Quo Vadis?** *(Via Lungo le Mura del Mandorlo 18, 0588-800.33; hours: 6:30PM–2AM)* is popular with the younger set. The wine bar **L'Incontro** *(Via Matteoti 18, 0588-805.00; call for hours)* also has good pastries and gelato. **Web & Wine** *(Via Porta all'Arco 11/19, 0588-815.31, www.webandwine.com; call for hours)* is an Internet café and wine bar.

WHERE TO SHOP

Alabaster objects and home decorations by regional artisans sell at **Gallerie Agostiniane** *(Piazza XX Settembre 3-5, 0588-868.68; call for hours)*. **Spartaco Montagnani** *(Via Porta all'Arco 6, 0588-861.84; call for hours)* creates bronze sculptures. **Camillo Rossi** *(Via Lungo le Mura del Mandorlo 7, 0588-861.33; call for hours)* produces fine alabaster pieces.

WHERE TO STAY

Once a convent, Hotel San Lino (€) *(Via San Lino 26, 0588-852.50, www.hotelsanlino.com)* offers comfort, a pool, and a cloister. Rustic Villa Nencini (€-€€€) *(Borgo Santo Stefano 55, 0588-863.86, www.villanencini.it)* is a peaceful oasis within a park. Park Hotel Le Fonti (€€) *(Via di Fontecorrenti 5, 0588-852.19, www.parkhotellefonti. com)* combines modern comfort, Tuscan details, and great views. Hotel La Locanda (€€) *(Via Guarnacci 24-28, 0588-815.47, www.hotel-lalocanda.com)* has spacious rooms, original work by local artists, and pleasant common areas.

Many Renaissance artists came to Chianti to paint the archetypal Tuscan landscape. Gentle hills, wine estates, castles, and beautiful medieval towns add splendor to the gorgeous countryside. The scenic Florence–Siena route SS222, called the *Chiantigiana*, "Chianti Road," cuts through the region and, along with SS429 ("SS" stands for *Strada Statale*, "State Road"), leads to some of the most beautiful towns in Tuscany.

GREVE IN CHIANTI

Tourist Info: Ufficio Turistico *(Viale G. da Verrazzano 59, Greve, 055-854.6287; call for hours)*

PLACES TO SEE
Landmarks, Arts & Entertainment:

Lively **Greve in Chianti**, with its arcaded main square, is a beautiful Tuscan village. The nearby Renaissance villa and wine estate **Villa Vignamaggio** *(Via Petriolo 5, 055-854.661, www.vignamaggio.com)* was the birthplace in 1479 of Mona Lisa Gioconda, the model for da Vinci's famous painting. It's also the site where Kenneth Branagh's *Much Ado About Nothing* was filmed. The first red wine called "Chianti" was produced on the estate in 1404. Up a narrow winding road, you arrive at **Montefioralle**, a picturesque, serene 14th-century hilltop village with great views of the region. Off Route SS2 is the beautiful 11th-century abbey **Badia a Passignano** *(Strada Statale di Val d'Elsa, 055-807.1622; tours available; call for hours)*, surrounded by the Antinori wine estate. An impressive alley of cypresses and steps leads to the church. Inside are works by the Ghirlandaios and Il Passignano.

PLACES TO EAT & DRINK

La Cantinetta di Rignana (€€-€€€) *(in nearby Rignana, 055-852.601, www.lacantinettadirignana.it; call for hours, closed Tu)* offers great food and a country locale. **Mangiando Mangiando** (€-€€) *(Piazza Matteotti 80, 055-854.6372, www.mangiandomangiando.it; call for hours, closed M)* does excellent meat dishes. For salads, light meals, or gelato, try **Caffé Lepanto** (€) *(Piazza Matteotti 4)*. Montefioralle: Marvelous **La Taverna del Guerrino** (€€) *(Via Montefioralle 39, 055-853.106; call for hours, closed M, Tu, W lunch)* offers a warm, country experience.

WHERE TO SHOP

Macelleria Falorni *(Piazza Matteotti 69, 055-853.029, www.falorni.it; hours: M–Sa 8AM–1PM, 3:30PM–7:30PM, Su 10AM-1PM, 3:30PM-7PM)* excels in wines and gourmet foods.

WHERE TO STAY

Albergo Giovanni da Verrazzano (€€) *(Piazza Matteotti 28, 055-853.189, www.albergoverrazzano.it)* has nice rooms, a good restaurant, and a lovely terrace.

Farmhouse apartments at Casa Mezzuola (€–€€) *(Via S. Cresci 30, 055-854.4885, www.mezzuola.com)* are charming; the location and views are great. Podere Torre (€) *(Via di S. Cresci 29, 055-854.4714, www.greve-in-chianti.com/poderetorre.htm)* is practically submerged in roses; this *agriturismo* pampers guests. Castello di Lamole (€€) *(Via di Lamole, Lamole area, 0340-105.3116, www. castellodilamole.it)*, once a 13th-century fortress, is a maze of passageways and arches graced by beautiful rafters, stone walls, and granite floors.

CASTELLINA IN CHIANTI

Tourist Info: Ufficio Informazioni Turistiche *(Via Ferruccio 40, Castellina, 0577-741.392; hours: M–Sa 10AM–1PM, 3PM–7PM, Su 10AM–1PM)*

PLACES TO SEE
Landmarks, Arts & Entertainment:
The walls of the fortified town Castellina in Chianti were built by Brunelleschi. This is home to the Castello di Fonterutoli vineyards *(see page 169)*. To the west, the 6th-century B.C. tomb Ipogeo di Montecalvario is a marvelous ancient specimen, with passages leading to the burial chamber. On the road toward Pievasciata is the Parco Sculture del Chianti *(0577-357.151, www.chiantisculpture park.it; hours: April–Oct 10AM–sunset, Nov–Mar by appt)*, with sculptures by diverse artists.

PLACES TO EAT & DRINK
Tuscan classics at Albergaccio (€€–€€€) *(Via Fiorentina 63, 0577-741.042, www.albergacciocast.com; call for*

hours, closed W–Th lunch & Su) come with a refined modern twist. Or try **Antica Trattoria La Torre (€€)** *(Piazza del Comune 15, 0577-740.236, www.antica trattorialatorre.com; call for hours, closed F)* for typical Tuscan fare.

WHERE TO SHOP

Enoteca Le Volte *(Via Ferruccio 12, 0577-741.314, www.enotecalevolte.com; call for hours)* sells wines, oils, and related paraphernalia.

WHERE TO STAY

Palazzo Squarcialupi (€€) *(Via Ferruccio 22, 0577-741.186, www.palazzosquarcialupi.com)* looks out over rolling hills; spacious rooms are nicely furnished; the ancient cellars have become a lovely spa. The **Fattoria Tregole (€€)** *(Tregole 86 area, 0577-740.991, www.fattoria-tregole.com)* vineyard has country-style rooms with hand-stenciled walls and  brass beds. Isolated, romantic **Locanda le Piazze (€€)** *(Le Piazze area, 0577-743.190, www.locandalepiazze.it)*, engulfed in vineyards and lavender, is a sophisticated country villa. Converted peasant cottages nestled in hillside woods, **Tenuta di Ricavo (€€-€€€)** *(0577-740.221, www.ricavo.com)* is a stunningly beautiful, peaceful haven. **Hotel Belvedere di San Leonino (€€)** *(San Leonino area, 0577-740.887, www.hotelsanleonino.com)* is rustic and charming.

RADDA IN CHIANTI

Tourist Info: *(Piazza del Castello, 0577-738.494, www. raddainchiantilife.com; hours: M–Sa 10AM–1PM, 3PM– 7PM, Su 10AM–1PM)*

Radda in Chianti is a stunning medieval town with imposing stone houses and sloping streets. It was the capital of the League of Chianti, a medieval Florentine coalition of towns defending against Siena. The league's emblem, a black rooster *(gallo nero)*, is now a symbol for the Chianti wine consortium.

PLACES TO EAT & DRINK

Ristorante Vignale (€€-€€€) *(Via Pianigiani 9, 0577-738.094, www.vignale.it; call for hours)* is an elegant eatery that offers reinterpretations of traditional Tuscan recipes.

WHERE TO SHOP

Ceramiche Rampini *(Casa Beretone di Vistarenni, 0577-738.043, www.rampiniceramics.com; call for hours)* produces marvelous hand-painted ceramics. Much of the artwork was inspired by local flora and fauna.

WHERE TO STAY

Airy, comfortable **Palazzo Leopoldo** (€€-€€€) *(Via Roma 33, 0577-735.605, www.palazzoleopoldo.it)* has an indoor pool, a spa, and a good restaurant. Small, picturesque **Relais Vignale** (€€-€€€) *(Via Pianigiani 9, 0577-738.300, www.vignale.it)* fronts on the town but has country views in back; the wine shop and tastings are a plus. Podere Terreno (€€) *(Via della Volpaia, 0577-738.312, www.podereterreno.it)*, an *agriturismo* with a stone farmhouse, has a lake and gorgeous views. La Locanda (€€€) *(Montanino area, 0577-738.833, www.lalocanda.it)*, peacefully remote, with rafters, antiques, and stunning views, is tastefully rustic.

GAIOLE IN CHIANTI
Tourist Info: Pro Loco *(Via G. Galilei 11, Gaiole in Chianti, 0577-749.411; call for hours)*

PLACES TO SEE
Landmarks, Arts & Entertainment:
Located between **Radda** and **Gaiole in Chianti**, lies the winery **Badia a Coltibuono** *(Gaiole in Chianti, 0577-744.81, www. coltibuono.com)*, once a medieval abbey. It offers wine and olive oil tastings, cooking classes, and tours of the vineyards, olive mills, and winemaking facilities. South of

Gaiole in Chianti, the gardens and rampart walkway of **Castello di Brolio** *(0577-7301, www.ricasoli.it; hours: Mar–Nov 10AM–5:30PM, Dec gardens only Sa–Su 10AM–4PM, Jan–Feb by appt)*, a residence of the Ricasoli wine dynasty since the 11th century, are open to the public. From atop the parapet, the view is splendid, the **Barone Ricasoli** winery *(see page 169)* stretching out below.

PLACES TO EAT & DRINK

In the 700-year-old abbey-turned-winery **Badia a Coltibuono** (€€) *(Gaiole in Chianti, 0577-749.031, www.coltibuono.com; call for hours)*, the restaurant offers game and gorgeous gardens.

WHERE TO STAY

There are several wonderful renovated medieval castles near **Gaiole**: **Castello di Spaltenna** (€€€-€€€€) *(Via Spaltenna 13, 0577-749.483, www.spaltenna.it)*; **Castello di Meleto** (€€) *(0577-749.129, www.castellomeleto.it)*; and **Castello di Tornano** (€€-€€€€) *(0577-746.067, www.castelloditornano.it)*. A converted water mill, **L'Ultimo Mulino** (€€-€€€) *(La Ripresa di Vistarenni area, 0577-738.520, www.ultimomulino.it)* enchants with its high ceilings, stone walls, arches, and bridges. Owned by a former fashion designer, **Borgo Argenina** (€€-€€€€) *(Argenina area, 0577-747.117, www.borgoargenina.it)* is exquisite in every detail, from stenciled walls to handmade quilts; rentals include suites, house, and villa. Amid hills and olive groves, **Hotel Residenza San Sano** (€€) *(San Sano area, 0577-746.130, www.sansanohotel.it)* brings out the charm of its stone farmhouses. **Castelletto di Montebenichi** (€€€) *(Montebenichi area, 055-991.0110, www.castelletto.it)* is pure magic, a small fairy-tale castle in a medieval village.

NECTAR OF THE GODS: CHIANTI VINEYARDS

There is a plethora of vineyards in Tuscany, especially in the Chianti region. Listed below are some of the more prominent ones and their wine shops. For visits and tastings, call for an appointment.

Castello di Verrazzano *(Via San Martino in Valle 12, Greti, Greve in Chianti, 055-854.243, www.verrazzano.com).*

Castello di Fonterutoli *(Via Ottone III 5, Fonterutoli, Castellina in Chianti, 0577-735.71, www.fonterutoli.it).*

Barone Ricasoli *(Castello di Brolio, Gaiole in Chianti, 0577-730.1, www.ricasoli.it).*

Riecine *(Gaiole in Chianti, 0577-749.098, www.riecine.com).*

Castell'in Villa *(Castelnuovo Berardenga, 0577-359.074, www.castellinvilla.com).*

Info on Chianti vineyards: Consorzio Vino Chianti Classico *(055-822.85, www.chianticlassico.com).*

PANZANO IN CHIANTI
Tourist Info: *(www.panzano.com)*

The fortified town of **Panzano in Chianti** is now most often known for its famous butcher, Dario Cecchini. It's a small and often overlooked village, but it's a beautiful town with quality wine bars flowing with food and drink.

PLACES TO EAT & DRINK
Fabulous views at **Oltre il Giardino (€-€€)** *(Piazza G. Bucciarelli 42, 055-852.828, www.ristoranteoltreil giardino.it; call for hours, closed M)* are as sumptuous as the food portions. Wine bar **Enoteca Il Vinaio (€)** *(Via Santa Maria 22, 055-852.603; call for hours, closed Tu)* is good for a Tuscan meal.

WHERE TO SHOP
The leather goods at **Carlo Fagiani** *(Via G. da Verrazzano 17/19, 055-852.239, www.carlofagiani.com; hours: M–F 10AM–1PM, 3PM–7PM, Sa 11AM–1PM, 3:30PM–6:30PM, Su 11AM–1PM)* are ready-to-wear or custom-made.

WHERE TO STAY
Villa Sangiovese (€€) *(Piazza G. Bucciarelli 5, 055-852.461, www.villasangiovese.it)* is a lovely hotel on a square overlooking the countryside. Intimate, elegant **Villa Le Barone (€€€)** *(Via San Leolino 19, 055-852.621, www.villalebarone.com)* was the home of the noted della Robbia family; it is inviting, beautifully furnished, and sports a pool on a terrace above vineyards and a rose garden. In a cozy stone farmhouse, **Fagiolari (€€)** *(Case

Sparse 25, 055-852.351, www.fagiolari.it) has spacious rooms, chestnut-wood beams, and a pool among the cypresses; the owner gives cooking lessons.

NEARBY PLACES TO STAY

Monteriggioni: In a beautiful medieval town noted in Dante's *Inferno*, Hotel Monteriggioni (€€€) *(Via 1 Maggio 4, 0577-305.009, www.hotelmonteriggioni.it)* is a charming small hotel converted from a former stable. **Barberino Val d'Elsa:** Tucked into a cypress grove, Le Filigare (€-€€) *(San Donato in Poggio area, 055-807.2796, www.lefiligare.it, weekly rentals)* is a traditional Tuscan villa. Apartments at the wine estate Fattoria Casa Sola (€) *(Via Cortine 5, 055-807.5028, www.fattoriacasasola.com)* each have private entrances and gardens. Il Paretaio (€-€€) *(Strada delle Ginestre 12, 055-805.9218, www.ilparetaio.it)*, a horse ranch, offers riding outings and lessons.

MONTALCINO ★

Narrow winding streets, steep stairs, tiled rooftops atop one another, a dramatic hilltop position, and a 14th-century fortress make Montalcino an exceptionally beautiful medieval town. Its many wine bars reflect the importance of winemaking to the area.

Tourist Info: Ufficio Informazioni *(Costa del Municipio 1, 0577-849.331, www.prolocomontalcino.it; hours: 10AM–1PM, 2PM–5:40PM, to 5:50PM Apr–Oct)*

Info on Montalcino vineyards: Consorzio del Vino Brunello di Montalcino *(Piazza Cavour 8, Montalcino, 0577-848.246, www.consorziobrunellodimontalcino.it)*

PLACES TO SEE
Landmarks, Arts & Entertainment:

The ramparts of the **Fortezza** *(Piazzale della Fortezza, 0577-849.211)* are a fantastic spot for viewing the countryside. The center of town is **Piazza del Popolo**, dominated by the commanding **Palazzo Comunale** *(Costa del Municipio 1, closed Su)*. The fine **Museo Civico e Diocesano** *(Via Ricasoli 31, 0577-846.014; hours: Jan–Mar Tu–Su 10AM–1PM, 2PM–4PM, Apr–Dec Tu–Su 10AM–6PM)* houses, among other things, prehistoric and Etruscan artifacts, early ceramics, and art of the Sienese

School. The nearby former convent of **Sant'Agostino** is worth seeing for its lovely frescoes.

NEARBY PLACES TO SEE

South of Montalcino is **Abbazia di Sant'Antimo** *(Castelnuovo dell'Abate area, 0577-835.659, www. antimo.it; hours: M–Sa 10:15AM–12:30PM, 3PM–6:30PM, Su 9:15AM–10:45AM, 3PM–6PM)*, a splendid Benedictine abbey believed to have been founded by Charlemagne in 781. The present French Romanesque church dates from 1118—with a travertine exterior and alabaster interior—giving it a spiritual luminosity. Sunday mass is accompanied by Gregorian chant. North of Montalcino, the abbey **Abbazia di Monte Oliveto Maggiore** *(0577-707.611, www.monteolivetomaggiore.it; hours: 9:15AM–12PM, 3:15PM–5PM/6PM in summer)* is stunning outside and magnificently frescoed inside.

PLACES TO EAT & DRINK
Where to Eat:

Trattoria Sciame (€-€€) *(Via Ricasoli 9, 0577-848.017; hours: W–M 12PM–2:30PM, 7PM–9:30PM)*, small but popular, has local dishes like *pinci* pasta in wild boar sauce. **Re di Macchia** (€-€€) *(Via Saloni 21, 0577-846.116; call for hours, closed Th)* is another good choice.

Bars & Nightlife:

One of the best cellars and wine bars, the beautiful **Enoteca La Fortezza** *(Piazzale della Fortezza, 0577-849. 211, www.enotecalafortezza.com; hours: summer 9AM–8PM; winter 9AM–6PM)* is in the fortress itself. Historic

Fiaschetteria Italiana *(Piazza del Popolo 6, 0577-849.043, www.fiaschetteriaitaliana.it; call for hours)* is perfect for drinks, coffee, and people-watching.

NEARBY PLACES TO EAT & DRINK

Boccon DiVino **(€€-€€€)** *(Colombaio Tozzi area, 0577-848.233, www.bsur.it/boccondivino; call for hours, closed Tu)* has excellent food and stupendous views. **Taverna dei Barbi (€€)** *(Podernovi area, 0577-847.117, www.fattoria deibarbi.it; call for hours, closed W)* offers authentic local cuisine and country elegance. **Poggio Antico (€€€-€€€€)** *(I Poggi area, 0577-848.044, www.poggioantico.com; call for hours)* provides fine dining, an innovative menu, and lovely hill views.

WHERE TO SHOP

Enoteca La Fortezza *(see page 173)* has a fine selection of wines. **Giuliana Bernardini** *(Piazzale Fortezza 1, 0577-846.144; call for hours)* sells local crafts, especially housewares. For glassware and table linens, as well as wines, try **Montalcino 564** *(Piazza del Popolo 36, 0577-848.419, www.montalcino564.it; call for hours, closed Su in winter)* and their nearby clothing shop **Capalbio** *(Via Mazzini 25, 0577-849.109, call for hours, closed Su in winter)*.

WHERE TO STAY

Delightful **Giglio Hotel** **(€-€€)** *(Via S. Saloni 5, 0577-846.577, www.gigliohotel.com)* has open-faced brick walls, rafters, and frescoes. **Hotel Vecchia Oliviera (€€)** *(Porta Cerbaia, Angolo Via Landi 1, 0577-846.028, www.vecchiaoliviera.com)*, a rustic villa on the edge of town, has gorgeous views. **Agriturismo Le Ragnaie (€)** *(Le*

Ragnaie area, 0577-848.639, www.leragnaie.it) is a family-style farmhouse.

NEARBY PLACES TO STAY

San Giovanni d'Asso: Located in the town's castle, La Locanda del Castello (€€) *(Piazza Vittorio Emanuele II 4, 0577-802.939, www.lalocandadelcastello.com)* is a warm, inviting residence. Tastefully furnished Lucignanello Bandini (€€€-€€€€) *(Lucignano d'Asso area, 0577-803.068, www.borgolucignanello.com)* does weekly rentals of apartments and a villa. **Buonconvento**: Fattoria Pieve a Salti (€) *(0577-807.244, www.pieveasalti.it)* offers plenty of sporting activities in addition to a spa. La Ripolina (€) *(Pieve di Piana area, 0577-282.280, www.laripolina.it)*, a rustic farmhouse, is perched on a hill above vineyards and sunflower fields.

Pienza is named after its illustrious son, Pope Pius II Piccolomini, who commissioned architect Bernardo Rossellino to redesign it in 1458. It is an enchanting mix of Gothic and Renaissance beauty, encircled by ramparts, an appropriate location for films such as *Romeo and Juliet* and *The English Patient*. The nearby Orcia Valley, its gently undulating slopes sporadically dotted with cypresses, has a sublime beauty typical of many Renaissance paintings.

Tourist Info: Prospettiva Pienza–Ufficio Turistico *(Piazza D. Alighieri 18, 0578-748.359, www.ufficioturisticodi pienza.it and www.pienza.it; call for hours)*

PLACES TO SEE
Landmarks, Arts & Entertainment:

The **Duomo** *(Piazza Pio II)* contains several masterpieces: Vecchietta's painting of St. Agatha holding her severed breasts as Pope Pius blesses them, and Sano di Pietro's

Madonna and Saints. The pope's residence, **Palazzo Piccolomini** *(Piazza Pio II, 0578-748.392 or 0577-286.300, www.palazzopiccolominipienza.it; hours: Mar 15–Oct 15 Tu–Su 10AM–6:30PM, Oct 16–Nov 15, Dec 1–Jan 6, Feb 15–Mar 14 Tu–Su 10AM–4:30PM)*, has an arcaded courtyard, tiered loggia, and lovely garden. The **Museo Diocesano**

(Corso Rossellino 30, 0578-749.905; hours: mid-Mar–Oct W–M 10AM–1PM, 3PM–6PM; Nov–mid-Mar Sa–Su 10AM–1PM, 3PM–6PM) houses a collection of superb medieval and early Renaissance art.

NEARBY PLACES TO SEE

In the enchanting village of **Castiglione d'Orcia**, there are marvelous views of the Val d'Orcia from **Rocca a Tentennano** *(Tourist Office, Viale Marconi 13, 0577-887.363; hours: summer M–Sa 10AM–1PM, Su 10AM–1PM, 2:30PM–4:30PM; winter Sa 10AM–1PM)*, a fortress on a promontory. Equally charming, **San Quirico d'Orcia** surprises at every turn of its medieval streets: stone arch-ways, Gothic churches, the Romanesque-Gothic **Collegiata** *(Via Dante Alighieri, 0577-897.236; hours: 8AM–5PM)* and the **Horti Leonini** *(Piazza Libertà, 0577-897.211; hours: 8AM–8PM)*, a 16th-century garden.

Tourist Info: San Quirico d'Orcia *(Via Dante Alighieri 33, 0577-897.211; call for hours)*

Bagno Vignoni *(Tourist Info: 0577-887.365)*, once touted by the likes of St. Catherine of Siena and Lorenzo the Magnificent for its thermal waters, is a small gem. For spa service today, you have to go to **Hotel Posta Marcucci** *(0577-887.112, www.hotelpostamarcucci.it)* or **Terme San Filippo** *(Via San Filippo 23, 0577-872.982 reservations 0577-872.007, 11AM–1PM, www.termesanfilippo.it; closed Nov–mid-May)*. Drive the back roads of the area to explore its fabulous nooks and crannies. A few villages noteworthy for their extraordinary beauty and charm are **Cetona**, **Radicofani**, **Abbadia San Salvatore**, and **Arcidosso**.

PLACES TO EAT & DRINK
Where to Eat:
Trattoria Latte di Luna (€-€€) *(Via San Carlo 2/4, 0578-748.606; hours: W–M 12:20PM–2:20PM, 7:30PM–9:20PM, closed Feb–Mar 15 & July)* serves simple, rustic food. **La Buca delle Fate** (€-€€) *(Corso Rossellino 38a, 0578-748.272; call for hours, closed M)* offers local fare in a 15th-century palazzo with vaulted brick ceilings.

Bars & Nightlife:
La Taverna di Re Artu *(Via della Rosa 4, 0333-472.4966, www.latavernadireartu.com; hours: 10:30AM–8:30PM)* is a popular wine bar. For a change of tone, **Bar Il Casello** *(Via del Casello 3, 0578-749.105; open til 12AM)* is a modern café with good wines and late hours.

NEARBY PLACES TO EAT & DRINK
Monticchiello: Osteria La Porta (€-€€) *(Via del Piano 1, 0578-755.163, www.osterialaporta.it; call for hours, closed Th)* serves excellent regional dishes; the terrace has fabulous views of Val d'Orcia. **Bagno Vignoni:** In a lovely 14th-century building, **Antica Osteria del Leone** (€) *(Piazza del Moretto, 0577-887.300; call for hours, closed M)* specializes in homemade pasta, guinea fowl with *vin santo*, and game.

WHERE TO SHOP

Pienza is known for pecorino, or sheep's-milk cheese; the best is in shops along **Corso Rossellino** (read labels for authenticity). **Ceramiche della Mezzaluna** *(Piazza Dante 18, studio Via Gozzante 67, 0578-748.561; call for hours)*, a

ceramics shop, sells lovely tiles. Specialty foods are scrumptious at **La Bottega del Cacio** *(Corso Rossellino 66, 0578-748.713; hours: 9:30AM–1PM, 3PM–7:30PM)*. Fabulous wrought iron pieces at **Biagiotti Mario e Figli** *(facing Piazza Pio II, Via I Maggio 1, 0578-748.478, www.biagiottipienza.com; hours: 10AM–1PM, 3PM–7:30PM)* are inspired by ancient designs. Gorgeous handmade shoes and other leather goods are the trade of **Calzoleria Pientina** *(Via Gozzante 22, 0578-749.040; call for hours)*. **Enoteca di Ghino** *(Via del Leone 16, 0578-748.057/748.262, www.enotecadighino.it; hours: Apr–Oct 9AM–1PM, 2:30PM–7:30PM, Nov–Mar call for hours)* wine connoisseurs sell fine *vino*. The owner, Ghino Poggialini, will help you choose the perfect wine.

WHERE TO STAY

Once a 15th-century monastery, **Il Chiostro di Pienza** *(€€-€€€) (Corso Rossellino 26, 0578-748.400, www. relaisilchiostrodipienza.com)* is now a stunningly beautiful hotel with marble colonnades and stone arches. Franco Zeffirelli's *Romeo and Juliet* was filmed here, as was *The English Patient*. **Dal Falco** (€) *(Piazza Dante*

Alighieri 3, 0578-748.551, www.ristorantedalfalco.it), a small inn and restaurant, is a comfortable no-frills cheap sleep. San Gregorio Residence (€-€€) *(Via della Madonnina 4, 0578-748.059, www.sangregorioresidence hotel.it)* is comfortable and convenient.

NEARBY PLACES TO STAY

L'Olmo (€€-€€€) *(Monticchiello area, 0578-755.133, www.olmopienza.it)* is a little gem—refined and cozy. Le Traverse (€€-€€€) *(Le Traverse area, 0578-748.198, www.letraverse.it)* is a sophisticated country home, chic and intimate. **Castiglione d'Orcia:** Stay in farmhouses belonging to a medieval castle high on a hill at Castello di Ripa d'Orcia (€€) *(Ripa d'Orcia area, 0577-897.376, www.castelloripadorcia.com),* offering spectacular views, simple rooms, and fairy-tale surroundings.

Even from afar, Montepulciano bewitches. Stunningly beautiful, this medieval hill town, one of Tuscany's highest, extends along a peak above woods and lush valleys. Known for centuries for its fine Vino Nobile wines, Montepulciano is a decidedly Renaissance town despite its medieval walls. Its allegiance to Florence brought in Florentine architects, most notably Antonio da Sangallo the Elder, Vignola, and Michelozzo. Its steep streets, barred to cars, contain many notable artworks, both inside and outside the palazzi. In recent times, its beauty has drawn film directors to its slopes: *A Midsummer Night's Dream* was shot here, as was the wedding scene in *Under the Tuscan Sun.*

Tourist Info: Pro Loco *(Via Gracciano nel Corso 59a, 0578-757.341, www.prolocomontepulciano.it; hours: summer M–Sa 9:30AM–12:30PM, 3PM–8PM, Su 10AM–12:30PM; winter M–Sa 9:30AM–12:30PM, 3PM–6PM, Su 10AM–12:30PM)*

PLACES TO SEE
Landmarks, Arts & Entertainment:
Via di Gracciano nel Corso (locally called "Corso"), the main street, is lined with Renaissance buildings, most notably **Palazzo Bucelli** *(Via G. nel Corso 73; closed to*

public). Its 18th-century owner, Pietro Bucelli, had Etruscan funerary urns from his collection laid into the base. Don't let the unfinished façade of the **Duomo** *(Piazza Grande; hours: 8:30AM–1PM, 3PM–7PM)* fool you: masterpieces lie within—one of which is Bartolo's *Assumption of the Virgin.* **Palazzo Comunale** *(Piazza Grande 1, 0578-717.300; hours: M, W 9:30AM–5:30PM, Tu, Th–Sa 9:30AM–12:30PM),* the town hall, was revamped by Michelozzo in the 15th century. The view from its tower is fabulous. Sangallo's **Palazzo Tarugi** *(Piazza Grande; closed to public)* has a fabulous and famous well out front with griffins and lions atop Etruscan columns. Nearby, in **Palazzo Neri-Orselli**, the **Museo Civico** *(Via Ricci 10, 0578-717.300, www. museisenesi.org; hours: winter Tu-Su 10AM–1PM, 3PM–6PM; summer Tu–Su 10AM–7PM)* has fine archaeological specimens. The magnificent **Madonna di San Biagio** *(Via di San Biagio 14; hours: 9AM–12:30PM, 3PM–6PM, til 7PM in July–Aug, no phone),* Sangallo's *tour de force,* is a beautiful domed church outside the city walls.

WINERIES

For info on Montepulciano vineyards or to sample wine from member vineyards, visit **Consorzio del Vino Nobile di Montepulciano** *(Palazzo del Capitano, Piazza Grande 7, Montepulciano, 0578-757.812, www.vinonobiledimontepulciano.it or www.consorziovinonobile.it; shop hours: M–Sa 1PM–6PM)*.

HERE ARE A COUPLE OF OPTIONS:
Avignonesi (Le Cappezzine) *(0578-724.304, www.avignonesi.it; hours: M–F 9AM–6PM)*

Poliziano *(0578-738.171, www.carlettipoliziano.com)*

PLACES TO EAT & DRINK
Where to Eat:

Laid-back, popular **Diva e Maceo (€)** *(Via Gracciano nel Corso 90-92, 0578-716.951; call for hours, closed Tu)* drums up classics and local specialties. Among the Etruscan-based dishes at **Il Cantuccio (€-€€)** *(Via delle Cantine 1, 0578-757.870, www.ristoranteilcantuccio. com; call for hours, closed M)*, the duck is especially good. Rustic but snazzy, **Borgo Buio (€-€€)** *(Via Borgo Buio 10, 0578-717.497, www.borgobuio.it; call for hours, closed M)* has great snacks and good meals.

Bars & Nightlife:

Famous **Antico Caffè Poliziano (€€)** *(Via Voltaia nel Corso*

27, 0578-758.615, www.caffepoliziano.it; hours: 7AM–12AM) was a watering hole of Malaparte, Pirandello, and Fellini; the Art Deco café serves drinks, food, and snacks and has marvelous views. Sip wine in the cellars of a historical palazzo at **Contucci** *(Palazzo Contucci, Piazza Grande 13, 0578-757.006, www.residenzecontucci.it; call for hours)*. Another historic winery, **Gattavecchi** *(Santa Maria area, Via Collazzi 74, 0578-757.110, www.gattavecchi.it; call for hours)* occupies underground caves in a 12th-century convent. Listen to jazz and blues at charming **Caffè degli Archi** *(Vicolo San Cristofano 2, 0578-757.739; call for hours)*.

NEARBY PLACES TO EAT & DRINK

Toward Chianciano Terme: Fattoria Pulcino (€) *(Rte SS146, 0578-758.711, www.pulcino.com, call for hours)* does good country food at friendly communal tables. **Chianciano Terme: Patry (€–€€)** *(Viale G. Di Vittorio 80, 0578-630.14, www.ristorantepatry.it; hours: Tu–Su 12:30PM–2:30PM, 7:30PM–11PM)* is also a good fish restaurant; **Il Buco (€€)** *(Via della Pace 39, 0578-302.30; call for hours, closed W)*, a friendly pizzeria. **Montefollonico: La Chiusa (€€€€)** *(Via della Madonnina 88, 0577-669.668, www.ristorantelachiusa.it; call for hours, closed Tu; also hotel)*, one of the finest regional restaurants, serves creative Tuscan dishes. **San Biagio: La Grotta (€€-€€€)** *(Via San Biagio 15, 0578-757.607/479; call for hours, closed W)* is excellent; delicacies include Chianti beef, *bistecca alla fiorentina*, stuffed pigeon, and rabbit.

WHERE TO SHOP

Avignonesi *(Via G. nel Corso 91, 0578-757.872; hours: 10AM–1PM, 3PM–7PM)* sells fine wines and olive oil from its estates. The fabulous gold jewelry at **Aliseda** *(Via dell'Opio nel Corso 8, 0578-758.672; hours: 9:30AM–8PM, closed Su–M in summer)* adopts ancient motifs. **Maledetti Toscani** *(Via Voltaia nel Corso 40, 0578-757.130, www.maledettitoscani.com; hours: 10AM–8PM)* features handmade articles of leather, wrought iron, copper, and other materials. For handcrafted copperware, go to **Bottega del Rame** *(Via dell'Opio nel Corso 64, 0578-758.753, www.rameria.com; hours: 9:30AM–7:30PM).*

WHERE TO STAY

Albergo Il Marzocco (€) *(Piazza Savonarola 18, 0578-757.262, www.albergoilmarzocco.it)* has spacious rooms, simple but nice. Frescoed ceilings, wrought iron beds, and family antiques make **L'Agnolo** (€) *(Via Gracciano nel Corso 63, 0578-717.070)* a special B&B. **La Dionora** (€€€-€€€€) *(Via V. di Poggiano, 0578-717.496, www.dionora.it)* is a classy inn with well-appointed rooms. On a hilltop overlooking the church of San Biagio, **Montorio** (€€-€€€) *(Strada per Pienza 2, 0578-717.442, www.montorio.com)* is surrounded by vineyards, olive groves, and cypresses. **Hotel Il Borghetto** (€€) *(Via Borgo Buio 7, 0578-757.535, www.ilborghetto.it)* offers simple, charming rooms in a rustic 16th-century house with fabulous views.

NEARBY TOWN

CHIUSI
(southeast of Chianciano Terme)

Tourist Info: *(Piazza Duomo 1, 0578-227.667, www. siena.turismo.toscana.it or www.comune.chiusi.si.it; call for hours)*

PLACES TO SEE
Landmarks, Arts & Entertainment:

In **Chiusi**, an ancient Etruscan center, the **Museo Archeologico Nazionale** *(Via Porsenna 93, 0578-201.77; hours: 9AM–8PM)* houses an important collection of Etruscan artifacts. Most were dug up from the many local Etruscan burial grounds; the museum arranges tours to the tombs. To visit the **Porsenna Labyrinth**, an intricate system of underground galleries used in ancient times for water transport, inquire at the **Museo della Cattedrale** *(Piazza del Duomo, 0578-226.490; hours: June–mid-Oct 10AM–12:45PM, 4PM–6:30PM; mid-Oct–May M–F 10AM–12:30PM, holidays 10AM–12:30PM, 4PM–6PM)*.

PLACES TO EAT & DRINK

Chiusi offers plenty of restaurants: Family-run **Zaira** **(€-€€)** *(Via Arunte 12, 0578-202.60, www.zaira.it/ italiano.htm; call for hours, closed M in winter)* serves local cuisine; *pasta del lucumone* is ham baked in three cheeses. Under vaulted brick ceilings, **La Solita Zuppa (€-€€)** *(Via Porsenna 21, 0578-210.06, www.lasolitazuppa.it; hours: W–M 12:30PM–2:30PM, 7:30PM–9:45PM)* serves creative versions of regional classics; try the *lasagne al cinghiale* (lasagna with wild boar). For a snack, **Osteria Il Kantharos** (€) *(Via Porsenna 37/39, 0578-219.36; call for hours, closed M)* is lovely. Along the lake east of Chiusi, **La Fattoria (€-€€)** *(Via Lago di Chiusi, 0578-214.07, www.la-fattoria.it; call for hours)* specializes in fish.

WHERE TO STAY

Residenza Re Porsenna (€) *(Via E. Baldetti 37, 0578-219.22)* is a charming B&B. Clean, simple rooms enhance the friendly atmosphere of Albergo La Sfinge (€) *(Via Marconi 2, 0578-201.57, www.albergolasfinge.it).*

chapter 6

AREZZO AND EASTERN
TUSCANY

AREZZO AND EASTERN TUSCANY

A. AREZZO ★

B. CORTONA ★

C. VAL DI CHIANA REGION

D. SANSEPOLCRO

E. CASENTINO REGION

• SNAPSHOT •

Though the A1 highway runs through eastern Tuscany, it is a rather isolated area, with deep forests and tall mountains. John Milton mentions the mystical woods surrounding Vallombrosa monastery in *Paradise Lost*. Favored by hermits, saints, and monks, the region has produced geniuses like Michelangelo, Piero della Francesca, and Giorgio Vasari. It is here St. Francis is said to have received the *stigmata*. Arezzo and Cortona offer art and culture, while Monterchi, Monte San Savino, and Lucignano are among Tuscany's most appealing villages.

TOP PICK!

AREZZO ★

Places to See:
1. Piazza Grande
2. Pieve di Santa Maria
3. Via dei Pileati
4. Casa Museo Ivan Bruschi
5. Fortezza Medicea
6. Il Prato
7. Duomo
8. San Domenico
9. Casa di Vasari
10. National Museum of Medieval and Modern Art
11. San Francesco
12. Museo Archeologico Mecenate
13. Museo dell'Oro

Places to Eat & Drink:
14. La Buca di San Francesco
15. Miseria e Nobiltà
16. Sbarbacipolle
17. Trattoria Il Saraceno
18. I Tre Bicchieri
19. Caffè dei Costanti
20. Il Gelato
21. Costachiara
22. La Casina del Prato
23. Enoteca La Torre di Gnicche
24. Discoteca Grace

Where to Shop:
25. Arezzo Antiques Fair
26. Corso Italia
27. Uno A Erre
28. Busatti

Where to Stay:
29. Cavaliere Palace Hotel
30. Minerva
31. I Portici
32. La Corte del Re
33. Casa Volpi
34. Villa i Bossi
35. Val di Colle
36. Fattoria Montelucci
37. Borgo Iesolana
38. Relais San Pietro
39. Il Borro
40. Villa Cassia di Baccano
41. Casa Simonicchi

N

V. Guido Tarlati

0   0.125 mi

0   125 m

V. della Chimera

21
39
40

Vle. Perennio

V. San Domenico

V. Garibaldi

V. XX Settembre

9

8

V. Madonna Laura

13

27
30
36
37

V. San Lorentino

10

Piagga del Murelo

V. Sasoverde

7

Fortezza Medicea

V. Garibaldi

V. dell'Orto

V. Ricasoli

6

Parco il Prato

V. del Saracino

16

V. Gesalpino

3

V. Porta Buia

V. Cavour

Pza. S. Francesco

22

4 1

2

23

5

V. Leone Leoni

V. Petrarca

Pza. del Popolo

V. G. Monaco

19

11 14

28

32

V. Bruno Buozzi

41

V. Teta

V. Fra Guittone

Pza. Guido Monaco

20

Italia

V. Mazzini

15

17

V. Oberdan

V. Borgo S. Croce

V. Fontanella

29

18 26

31 Corso

V. Garibaldi

Vle. Matteotti

Pza. della Repubblica

24

Pza. Risorgimento

Roma

V. Margaritone

V. Aretino

V. Trente e Trieste

Train Station

Vle. Michelangelo

V. Spinello

V. F. Crispi

Anfiteatro Romano

12

V. Guadagnoli

Vle. Luca Signorelli

38

33
34
35

V. Giotto

191

Arezzo, about 50 miles southeast of Florence, was an important hub and military outpost for the Etruscans and later the Romans. The town was home to Guido Monaco, 11th-century inventor of modern musical notation, 14th-century poet Petrarch, 16th-century architect Giorgio Vasari, author of the world's first art history book, *Lives of the Artists*, and today's Roberto Benigni, director and star of *Life Is Beautiful*. By the 1st century, Arezzo had become an industrial center specializing in embossed pottery. Today's *Arentines* are known for their gold jewelry and textiles. The city's industrial outskirts belie a restored historical center with myriad activities and sights. In June and September, a costumed medieval horseback joust is the focus of its famous **La Giostra del Saracino** *(Piazza Grande, 0575-377.462, www.giostradelsaracino.arezzo.it, second to last Sa of June, first Su of Sep)*, "Joust of the Saracens."

Summer music fest **Arezzo Wave** *(0575-401.722, July, www.arezzowave.com)* showcases rock, jazz, pop, funk, heavy metal, and classical, with some theater, comedy, and literature.

Tourist Info: APT *(Piazza della Repubblica 28, 0575-377.678, www.apt.arezzo.it; hours: Apr–Sep M–Sa 9AM–1PM, 3PM–7PM, Su 9AM–1PM; Oct–Mar M–Sa 9AM–1PM, 3PM–6:30PM, 1st Su of month 9AM–1PM)*

PLACES TO SEE
Landmarks, Arts & Entertainment:
One of Italy's most famous city squares, sloped **Piazza**

Grande (1) is renowned for its many architectural styles. On one side is the **Pieve di Santa Maria (2)** *(Corso Italia 7, 0575-226.29; hours: 8AM–1PM, 3PM–6:30PM)*, a Romanesque church with several arcade levels. The multi-arched campanile, or bell tower, is known as the "Tower of a Hundred Holes." The street fronting the church, **Via dei Pileati (3)**, is a jumble of Gothic towers and palazzi. **Casa Museo Ivan Bruschi (4)** *(Corso Italia 14, 0575-354.126 or 0575-3371; hours: Tu–Su 10AM–6PM; winter Tu–Su 9AM–1PM, 2PM–6PM)*, home of the late **Arezzo Antiques Fair (25)** *(see page 196)* founder, is packed with collectibles. **Fortezza Medicea (5)** *(hours: summer 7AM–8PM, winter 7:30AM–6PM)*, built by the Medici, offers wonderful views, as does the surrounding park **Il Prato (6)**.

Discover stained-glass windows by Guillaume de Marcillat and a Piero della Francesca fresco of Mary Magdalene at the **Duomo (7)** *(Piazza Duomo, 0575-239.91; hours: 7AM–12:30PM, 3PM–6:30PM)*. Gothic **San Domenico (8)** *(Piazza San Domenico, 0575-232.55; hours: 8:30AM–1PM, 3:30PM–7PM)* contains a compelling Crucifix painting by Cimabue. **Casa di Vasari (9)** *(Via XX Settembre 55, 0575-409.040; hours: M, W–Sa 9AM–7PM, Su 9AM–1PM)* is graced with works by Vasari and his contemporaries. The **National Museum of Medieval and Modern Art (10)** *(Museo Statale d'Arte Medievale e Moderna, Via di San Lorentino 8, 0575-409.050; hours: Tu–Su 8:30AM–7:30PM)* exhibits works by Vasari, Signorelli, among others, plus an outstanding *majolica* collection. **San Francesco (11)** *(Piazza San*

Francesco, church 0575-206.30, reservations required to view frescoes (Capella Bacci): 0575-352.727 or 0575-299.071, www.pierodellafrancesca.it; hours: church 8:30AM–6:30PM; Capella Bacci Apr–Oct M–F 9AM–6:30PM, Sa 9AM–5:30PM, Su 1PM–5:30PM; Nov–Mar M–F 9AM–5:30PM, Sa 9AM–5PM, Su 1PM–5PM) contains Piero della Francesca's fresco cycle masterpiece *The Legend of the True Cross.*

Highlights of the **Museo Archeologico Mecenate (12)** (*Via Margaritone 10, 0575-208.82; hours: 8:30AM–7:30PM*) include Etruscan objects and Roman-era Aretine pottery. The museum building overlooks the ruins of a **Roman amphitheater** (*hours: summer 7AM–8PM, winter 7:30AM–6PM*). Fabulous jewelry is on display at the **Museo dell'Oro (13)** (*Uno A Erre, Via Fiorentina 550, 0575-925.984, www.unoaerre.it; hours: M–F 9AM–6PM, Sa 9AM–1PM*) on the outskirts of the town.

PLACES TO EAT & DRINK
Where to Eat:

Set in an atmospheric frescoed cellar, **La Buca di San Francesco (14)** (€-€€) (*Via San Francesco 1, 0575-232.71, www.bucadisanfrancesco.it; call for hours*) does Tuscan classics in large portions. In another marvelous medieval setting, **Miseria e Nobiltà (15)** (€€) (*Via Piaggia di San Bartolomeo 2, 0575-212.45, arezzomiseriae nobilta.blogspot.com; hours: Tu–Su 7PM–11:30PM*) turns out local specialties. Deli **Sbarbacipolle (16)** (€) (*Via Garibaldi 120, 0575-299.154; hours: 7:30AM–8PM, closed 3 wks Aug*) is the spot for cold platters and *panini.*

Family-run **Trattoria Il Saraceno (17)** (€€) *(Via Mazzini 6, 0575-276.44, www.ilsaraceno.com; hours: Th–Tu 12:30PM–3PM, 7PM–11PM)* serves everything from Chianina beef to wild boar to wood-oven pizza. Embark on gustatory adventure at innovative **I Tre Bicchieri (18)** (€€€) *(Piazzetta Sopra i Ponti 3-5, 0575-265.57, www.itrebicchieri.it; hours: M–Sa 12:30PM–2PM, 7PM–10PM).* Old-fashioned **Caffè dei Costanti (19)** (€) *(Piazza San Francesco 19-20, 0575-182.4075; hours: summer Tu–Su 7AM–12AM, winter till 7:30PM)* was featured in the film *Life Is Beautiful.* Crowd-pleasing **Il Gelato (20)** (€) *(Via de' Cenci 24, 0575-300.069, hours: Th–Tu 11AM–12AM, winter Th–Tu 11AM–8PM)* offers lots of ice cream flavors. **Terranuova Bracciolini:** A meal is a vacation in itself at country restaurant **Costachiara (21)** (€€) *(Loc. Badiola, Via Santa Maria 129, 055-944.318, www.costachiara.it; hours: M 12:30PM–2PM, W–Su 12:30PM–2:30PM, 7:30PM–10PM; closed 3 wks Aug, 3 wks Jan).* Come hungry.

Bars & Nightlife:

Summer crowds at **La Casina del Prato (22)** *(Via Palagi 1, Il Prato park, 0575-299.757; hours: 10AM–2AM, winter W–M 10AM–2AM)* spill out into the surrounding park. Wine bar **Enoteca La Torre di Gnicche (23)** *(Piaggia San Martino 8, 0575-352.035; hours: Th–Tu 12PM–3PM, 6PM–1AM)* uncorks great vintages and serves good food. **Discoteca Grace (24)** *(Via Madonna del Prato 129, 0575-403.669; hours: Sep–May F–Sa 12AM–dawn)* caters to the dance-minded.

WHERE TO SHOP

Attracting collectors and bargain hunters from around the world, the monthly **Arezzo Antiques Fair (25)** *(Piazza Grande; 1st Su of month & preceding Sa)* combines flea market fare with antiques and crafts. Jewelry

shoppers converge on Arezzo's main retail thoroughfare, **Corso Italia (26)**, for gold and fine jewelry. Buy gold jewelry directly from the manufacturer at **Uno A Erre (27)** *(Via Fiorentina 550, 0575-9251, 800-801.196, www.unoaerre.it; call for hours, M–Sa)*; don't miss its jewelry museum **Museo dell'Oro (13)** *(see page 194)*. You'll find top-quality home fabrics and textiles at **Busatti (28)** *(Corso Italia 48, 0575-355.295, www.busatti.com; hours: M 3:30PM–7:30PM, Tu–Sa 9AM–1PM, 3:30PM–7:30PM)*.

WHERE TO STAY

Four-star **Cavaliere Palace Hotel (29)** (€€) *(Via Madonna del Prato 83, 0575-268.36, www.cavalierehotels.com)* offers modern accommodations, as does **Minerva (30)** (€€) *(Via Fiorentina 4, 0575-370.390, www.hotel-minerva.it)*, which also has a fitness center. Flamboyant **I Portici (31)** (€€-€€€) *(Via Roma 18, 0575-403.132, www.hoteliportici.com)* is a former private home; its ristorante is known for its cuisine. **La Corte del Re (32)** (€) *(Via Borgunto 5, 0575-401.603, www.lacortedelre.com; weekly rates)* offers equipped apartments, some overlooking Piazza Grande. On the outskirts of town, **Casa Volpi (33)** (€) *(Le Pietre area, Via Simone Martini 29, 0575-354.364, www.casavolpi.it)* offers country-style lodgings with wood beams and wrought-iron beds. Sign up for a cooking class during your stay at garden-surrounded Villa i Bossi (34) (€€) *(Loc. Gragnone 44-46, 0575-365.642, www.villaibossi.com).*

NEARBY PLACES TO STAY

Bagnoro Arezzo: Five minutes from town, Val di Colle (35) (€€€-€€€€) *(0575-365.157, www.valdicolle.it)* combines the best features of an old stone farmhouse with modern amenities. **Pergine Valdarno:** Get away from it all at country estate Fattoria Montelucci (36) (€) *(Le Ville area, 0575-896.525, www.montelucci.com),* "Mountain of Light." **Bucine:** Amid cypresses and olive trees, Borgo Iesolana (37) (€€-€€€€) *(Iesolana area, 055-992.988, www.iesolana.it)* offers a pool, cooking classes, and renovated stone farmhouses with modern furnishings. **Castiglion Fiorentino:** Relais San Pietro (38) (€€€) *(Polvano area, 0575-650.100, www.polvano.com, open Mar–Oct)* provides luxurious simplicity with panoramic views from a hilltop location. **San Giustino Valdarno:** Indulge in a stay at Ferragamo-owned estate Il Borro (39) (€€€-€€€€) *(055-977.053, www.ilborro.com),* set in a medieval village with vineyards and olive groves. Villa Cassia di Baccano (40) (€€-€€€) *(Via Setteponti Levante 132, 055-977.2310, www.villacassiadibaccano.it)* offers modern elegance in a 16th-century mill and villa. **Caprese Michelangelo:** Rooms at charming Casa Simonicchi (41) (€-€€) *(Via Simonicchi 184, 0575-793.762, www.simonicchi.com)* look out onto a picturesque garden.

When the book *Under the Tuscan Sun* and its film version were released, ancient Cortona became a major tourist destination. Founded by the Etruscans in 8th century B.C., the hillside city is a layer cake of civilizations. Medieval houses jut out at all angles along steep thoroughfares; the street name *Vicolo del Precipizio*, "Precipice Alley," says it all. Cortona is also known as being the birthplace of temperamental Renaissance painter Luca Signorelli. In August, its **Tuscan Sun Festival** (*www.tuscansunfestival.com*) attracts top conductors and singers, as does the **Sagra della Bistecca** (*Aug 14–15*), "Beef Steak Festival," highlighting the area's flavorful Chianina beef.

Tourist Info: APT (*Via Nazionale 42, 0575-630.353, www.cortonaweb.net; hours: May–Sep M–Sa 9AM–1PM, 3PM–6:30PM, Su 9AM–1PM; Oct–Apr M–F 9AM–1PM, 3PM–6PM, Sa 9AM–1PM*)

PLACES TO SEE
Landmarks, Arts & Entertainment:

Piazza del Duomo offers magnificent views of the valley below. A lovely spot from which to appreciate Cortona is from the top of the steps of the **Palazzo Comunale** (*Piazza della Repubblica*), the Town Hall. In the **Casali Palace** next door, the Etruscan Museum, **Museo dell'Accademia Etrusca** (*Palazzo Casali, Piazza Signorelli 9, 0575-637.248, www.accademia-etrusca.org; hours:*

Apr–Oct 10AM–7PM; Tu–Su 10AM–5PM Nov–Mar), houses extraordinary artifacts, including a bronze chandelier from the 4th century B.C. **Museo Diocesano** *(Piazza del Duomo 1, 0575-628.30; hours: Apr–Oct 10AM–7PM; Nov–Mar Tu–Su 10AM–5PM)* holds other masterpieces: Fra Angelico's *Annunciation* and works by Signorelli and Pietro Lorenzetti. The medieval houses along **Via Janelli** are among Italy's oldest.

Halfway up the slope toward the Medici Fortress is little **San Niccolò** *(off Via Berrettini, ring for custodian; hours: usually 9AM–12PM, 3PM–7PM; off-season 9AM–12PM, 3PM–5PM)*, with its two-sided Signorelli altarpiece *(ask custodian to display 2nd side)*. Further up, from outside the church of **Santa Margherita** and the **Fortezza Medicea** *(hours: Apr–May, June, Sep 10 AM–6 PM; July–Aug till 7PM)*, there are stupendous views of Cortona and the valley. Back down the slope, at **Piazza Garibaldi**, the photo-op view is of **Santa Maria delle Grazie** *(Calcinaio, 2 mi away; hours: opened at request of caretaker)*.

Etruscan tombs *(2 miles s. of Cortona, in the valley)* include the circular **Tanella di Pitagora** *(Maestà del Sasso, on road to Sodo, 0575-630.415; book in advance at Etruscan Museum)*, which is not for Pythagoras (the misnomer derives from confusion between Cortona and Crotone, the mathematician's birthplace), and the marvelous **Melone I** and **II tombs**, or "Il Sodo," marked by melon-shaped mounds. Ask at the APT tourist office and the Etruscan Museum *(see page 198)* about visiting Cortona's **Parco Archeologico**.

PLACES TO EAT & DRINK
Where to Eat:

Nouvelle at **Preludio** (€€) *(Via Guelfa 11, 0575-630.104, www.ilpreludio.net; call for hours, closed Nov–May on M & for lunch)* includes plum gnocchi with onions and porcini sauce. Stone-lined **La Grotta** (€–€€) *(Piazza Baldelli 3, 0575-630.271; hours: W–M 12PM–2:30PM, 7PM–10PM)* dishes up home-cooked crowd-pleasers. It's said Pope John Paul II once asked the chef at **Tonino** (€€) *(Piazza Garibaldi 1, 0575-630.500, www.ristorante tonino.com; hours: 12:30PM–2:30PM, 7:30PM–9:30PM)* to prepare his Christmas dinner. You'll love the views from its terrace. Locals like the homemade favorites at **Trattoria Dardano** (€) *(Via Dardano 24, 0575-601.944, www.trattoriadardano.com; call for hours, closed W)*; roasts are the specialty. **Il Falconiere** (€€€–€€€€) *(Loc. San Martino 370, 0575-612.679, www.ilfalconiere.com; call for hours, see hotel information on page 201)* is one of *Toscana's* must-do gastronomic experiences. Artfully prepared cuisine is presented in a glass-and-wrought-iron *limonaia* among cypress and olive trees.

Bars & Nightlife:

Enjoy live music at wine bar **La Saletta** *(Via Nazionale 26-28, 0575-603.366, www.caffelasaletta.it; hours: May–Oct 7:20AM–2AM, Nov–Apr closed W)*. Film stars once favored friendly **Caffè degli Artisti** *(Via Nazionale 18, 0575-601.237, www.cortonashop.com/caffart; hours: summer 7AM–2AM; winter closed Th & Nov)*. Irish pub **The Lion's Well** *(Piazza Signorelli 28, 0575-604.918; call for hours)* is a hit with 20- and 30-somethings.

WHERE TO SHOP

Shop for locally grown specialties and crafts at the **Farmers' Market** *(Palazzo Casali, 0575-630.610; Sa AM)*. **Il Cocciaio** *(Via Nazionale 69, 0575-601.246; call for hours)* sells Cortona's green, yellow, and cream-colored ceramics and reproductions of medieval Tuscan pottery. Another good ceramics shop: **Giulio Lucarini** *(Via Nazionale 54, 0575-604.405, www.terrabruga.com; call for hours)*.

WHERE TO STAY

Hotel Italia (€) *(Via Ghibellina 5-7, 0575-630.254, www.hotelitaliacortona.com)* provides spacious rooms and a rooftop terrace with far-flung views. Romantic **Hotel San Michele** (€€-€€€) *(Via Guelfa 15, 0575-604.348, www.hotelsanmichele.net)* is set in a medieval palazzo. Four-star **Hotel Villa Marsili** (€€-€€€) *(Viale C. Battisti 13, 0575-605. 252, www.villamarsili.net)* welcomes you with luxurious rooms and suites.

NEARBY PLACES TO STAY

Localita San Martino: Renowned **Relais Il Falconiere** (€€€-€€€€) *(Loc. San Martino 370, 0575-612.679, www.ilfalconiere.com)* is a converted 17th-century home, with antiques, fireplaces, and a celebrated restaurant *(see page 200)*. **Localita San Pietro a Cegliolo:** The quaint stone houses of Falconiere estate peasants have been converted into rustic apartments at **Borgo Elena** (€) *(Loc. San Pietro a Cegliolo, 0575-604.773, 3-night min)*; its pool offers panoramic views. **Creti:** Former farmhouse **Casa Bellavista** (€€) *(0575-610.311, www.casabellavista.it)* offers large, elegantly simple rooms with views, plus cooking lessons, bikes, Vespas, and balloon tours.

VAL DI CHIANA REGION (C)

The *Val di Chiana* (Chiana Valley) produces the white and gray Chianina cattle from which *bistecca alla fiorentina* is made. Its medieval towns Monte San Savino, Lucignano, and Foiano della Chiana are among Tuscany's most beautiful villages.

MONTE SAN SAVINO

Tourist Info: APT *(Piazza Gamurrini 25, 0575-849.418; www.comune.monte-san-savino.ar.it; hours: Apr–Oct Tu 9AM–1PM, W–F 9AM–1PM, 4PM–7PM Sa–Su 9AM–1PM, 2:30PM–7:30PM; Nov–Mar W–F 9AM–1PM, Sa–Su 9AM–1PM, 4PM–7PM).*

PLACES TO SEE
Landmarks, Arts & Entertainment:

Monte San Savino is a mix of medieval and Renaissance buildings. Its most prominent citizen was architect/sculptor Andrea Contucci, known as Andrea Sansovino, who designed the Classic-style **Loggia dei Mercanti** *(Corso Sangallo)*. His peer, Antonio da Sangallo the Elder, designed **Palazzo Comunale** *(Corso Sangallo)*, with an arcaded courtyard and open-air theater, for Cardinal Antonio di Monte. View local art in **Museo del Cassero** *(Piazza Gamurrini 25, 0575-849.418; hours: by appt).*

PLACES TO EAT & DRINK

Tempting Tuscan delights await on the lively terrace of **La Terrasse** (€€) *(Via di Vittorio 2-4, 0575-844.111, www.ristorantelaterrasse.it; call for hours, closed W).*

WHERE TO SHOP

Ceramiche Artistiche Lapucci *(Corso Sangallo 8-10, 0575-844.375; call for hours, closed Su, ring bell)* sells local pottery with floral designs.

WHERE TO STAY

Castello di Gargonza (€€) *(Loc Gargonza, 0575-847.021, www.gargonza.it)* is an entire medieval village turned into residence vacation and B&B-style lodging.

LUCIGNANO

Tourist Info: *(www.comune.lucignano.ar.it)*

PLACES TO SEE
Landmarks, Arts & Entertainment:

Lovely Lucignano is noted for its medieval town plan, consisting of four elliptical rings of streets. The **Collegiata** *(Costa San Michele, 0575-836.122; call for hours)* has a similarly concentric staircase. **Museo Comunale** *(Palazzo Comunale, Piazza del Tribunale 22, 0575-838.001; hours: Oct–Mar M 10AM–1PM, W–F 10AM–1PM, 2PM–5PM, Sa–Su 10AM–1PM, 2PM–6PM; Apr–Sep M, W–F 10AM–5PM, Sa–Su 10AM–6PM)* houses, among other works, an eight-foot gold, bejeweled reliquary—the *Tree of St. Francis*, or *Tree of Lucignano*.

PLACES TO EAT & DRINK

Il Goccino (€€) *(Via G. Matteotti 90, 0575-836.707, www.ilgoccino.it; call for hours, closed M in winter)* is known for its food and wine. Or try fried eggs with truffles at **La Rocca (€€)** *(Via G. Matteotti 15-17, 0575-836.775; call for hours, closed Tu).*

FOIANO DELLA CHIANA
Tourist Info: *(Galleria Furio del Furia, Via Solferino 9, 0575-649.928; www.foianoturismo.com; hours: M, Th, Sa 10AM–12:30PM)*

PLACES TO SEE
Landmarks, Arts & Entertainment:

With its archways and passageways, red-bricked **Foiano della Chiana** *(www.comune.foiano.ar.it)* surprises at every turn. Its **Collegiata di San Martino** *(Piazza della Collegiata, 0575-648.384; call for hours)* contains a terra-cotta Madonna by Andrea della Robbia and the last work by Signorelli, *Coronation of the Virgin.* Gallery **Fototeca Furio del Furia** *(Palazzo delle Logge, Piazza Cavour 7, 0575-648.888; hours: 8AM–2PM, 4PM–6PM)* exhibits fascinating early 20th-century photographs of Tuscan life. The town's celebrated **Carnavale** *(Jan/Feb, office: Corso V. Emanuele 35, 0575-642.100, www.carnevaledifoiano.it),* dating from 1593, is among Italy's oldest.

NEARBY PLACES TO STAY

Civitella in Val di Chiana: Relax at convivial **Casale Il Caggio (€€)** *(Loc. Ciggiano, Via del Caggio 15, 0575-440.022, www.agriturismo.com/ilcaggio),* an *agriturismo* in a rustic stone house. Near **Sinalunga:** For a fairy-tale Tuscan experience, consider **Locanda dell'Amorosa (€€€-€€€€)** *(Loc. L'Amorosa, 0577-677.211, www.amorosa.it),* a tiny hamlet transformed into luxury resort.

SANSEPOLCRO (D)

Medieval Sansepolcro, birthplace of painter Piero della
Francesca, is home to several of his major works, as well
as those of other artists.

Tourist Info: APT *(Via Matteotti 8, 0575-740.536,
www.apt.arezzo.it; hours: 9:30AM–1PM, 3:30PM–6:30PM)*

PLACES TO SEE
Landmarks, Arts & Entertainment:
The town's **Museo Civico** *(Palazzo Comunale, Via Aggiunti
65, 0575-732.218, www.museocivicosansepolcro.it; hours:
mid-Sep–mid-June 9:30AM–1PM, 2:30PM–6PM; mid-
June–mid-Sep 9:30AM–1:30PM, 2:30PM–7PM)* houses
della Francesca's acclaimed *Resurrection* and *Madonna
della Misericordia*. Piero inserted his image in both
pieces, as a soldier at Christ's resurrection and as one of
the faithful under the cloak of a powerful Madonna.
Rosso Fiorentino's *Deposition* is in **San Lorenzo** *(Via Santa
Croce, 0575-740.536; hours: 10AM–1PM, 3PM–6PM)*.
Check out the **loggia** *(Piazza San Francesco)* decorated
with skeletons and skulls; it's next to the church of Santa
Maria delle Grazie. Admire the interesting mix of mansions and medieval towers along **Via XX Settembre**.
Unique to the town: **Palio della Balestra** *(second Su Sep)*,
a Renaissance-costumed crossbow tournament.

PLACES TO EAT & DRINK
Sansepolcro mainstay **Ristorante Fiorentino** (€–€€) *(Via L.
Pacioli 60, 0575-742.033, www.ristorantefiorentino.it;*

call for hours, closed W) has been serving authentic Tuscan dishes since 1807. Elegant **Il Convivio (€-€€)** *(Via Traversari, Palazzo Bourbon del Monte, 0575-736.543; call for hours, closed Tu)* specializes in fine Apennine cuisine. Wine bar **Enoteca Guidi (€)** *(Via L. Pacioli 44, 0575-741.086, www.locandaguidi.it; call for hours, closed W, Sa, & lunch Su)* serves good food.

WHERE TO STAY

Albergo Fiorentino (€) *(Via L. Pacioli 56, 0575-740.350, www.albergofiorentino.com)* offers comfortable rooms with bath, shower, and AC; bike/scooter rentals available. Well-appointed **Borgo Palace Hotel (€-€€)** *(Via Senese Aretina 80, 0575-736.050, www.borgopalace.it)* has a renowned *ristorante*.

NEARBY TOWN

The hilltop hamlet of **Monterchi** *(between Arezzo and Sansepolcro)* is surrounded by sunflower fields and olive groves. Its *Mons Erculis*, "Hill of Hercules," was revered by Etruscans and Romans. The village boasts an art "must-see"—*Madonna del Parto*, a Piero della Francesca

painting depicting a pregnant Madonna, in its **Museo Madonna del Parto** *(Via Reglia 1, 0575-707.13; hours: Apr–Oct 9AM–1PM, 2PM–7PM, till 5PM Nov–Mar)*. Enjoy a bite in part of the town's old fortress at **Ristorante Al Travato (€€)** *(Piazza Umberto I 20, 0575-701.11; call for hours, closed M)*.

CASENTINO REGION (E)

Located in northeastern Tuscany, the Casentino region is rich in vegetation and ancient forests. There are many interesting villages that dot the region, such as Camáldoli, Poppi, Bibbiena, and Pratovecchio—all nestled in and around *Foresti Casentini* (the national park).

Tourist Info: *(Via Roma 203, Ponte a Poppi, 0575-520.511, www.turismo.casentino.toscana.it; hours: M–F 8AM–6PM)*

PLACES TO SEE
Landmarks, Arts & Entertainment:
For centuries, the ancient foothills, forests, and mountains of Tuscany's **Casentino Region** provided refuge for monks and mystics; the most famous to have trod the area was St. Francis. Today, hikers and mushroom hunters have all but replaced the holy men; still, *Foresti Casentini* remains home of the **Camáldoli Monastery** *(Convento, 0575-556. 012, www.camaldoli.it; hours: 9AM–1PM, 2:30PM–7PM, summer till 7:30PM)* and **Hermitage** *(Eremo, 0575-556. 021; hours: summer 9AM–12PM, 3PM–6PM, winter M–Sa 9AM–12PM, 3PM–5PM)*. Founded by St. Romuald in 1012, its setting and monastic village are spectacular. About 40 Carthusian monks reside here today; a small pharmacy sells soaps, liqueurs, and other items they produce. Art lovers should not miss the hermitage's Baroque church.

Towering over the town of **Poppi**, 13th-century Gothic castle **Castello dei Conti Guidi** *(Piazza Repubblica 1, 0575-520.516; hours: summer 10AM–7PM, winter Th–Su*

10AM–5PM, or by appt) is known for its views, frescoes, and historic library. It's said Dante once stayed here. Outside **Poppi**, Romanesque 12th-century **Pieve di Romena** *(Pratovecchio road)* features unique stone capitals. The now-ruined **Castello di Romena** *(Pratovecchio, under renovation)* appears in Dante's *Inferno*.

Despite its industrial surrounds, **Bibbiena** *(Tourist Info: Bibbiena train station, Via Rignano 17A, 0575-593.098)* remains a lovely walled town. Its **Pieve di Santi Ippolito e Donato** *(Piazza Tarlati; hours: 8AM–12PM, 3–7PM)* has an altarpiece by Bicci di Lorenzo. **San Lorenzo** *(Via Dovizi)* contains della Robbia's *Adoration of the Shepherds*. Across the street: **Palazzo Dovizi** *(Via Dovizi 26-28)* was the mansion of Bernardo Dovizi, or Cardinal Bibbiena, author of Italy's first Italian theatrical comedy, *La Calandria*, in 1513. On a mountainside east of **Bibbiena**, you'll find monastery **La Verna** *(0575-5341; hours: 7AM–7PM)*, founded by St. Francis. Here in 1224, the saint received *stigmata*, the markings of Christ's wounds. The monastery contains some of St. Francis's possessions, plus della Robbia terra cottas.

PLACES TO EAT & DRINK

Area dining options include **Poppi's Antica Cantina (€-€€)** *(Via Lapucci 2, 0575-529.844, www.anticacantina.com; call for hours, closed M)*, "Old Wine Cellar," serving flavorful fare. **Bibbiena's Il Tirabusciò (€)** *(Via Borghi 73, 0575-595.474, www.tirabuscio.it; hours: M lunch, W–Su lunch & dinner)* prepares local specialties with fresh seasonal ingredients.

WHERE TO STAY

In **Poppi**, three-star hotel Casentino Albergo-Ristorante (€) *(Piazza della Repubblica 6, 0575-529.090, www.albergo casentino.it)* has a garden and restaurant. Outside **Bibbiena**: An agritourist's delight, farm complex Agricola Casentinese (€) *(Loc. Casanova 63, 0575-594.806, www. agricolacasentinese.it)* boasts a herd of prize cattle, horses, a pool, and restaurant.

chapter 7

GROSSETO AND
SOUTHERN TUSCANY

GROSSETO AND SOUTHERN TUSCANY

1. MASSA MARITTIMA
2. POPULONIA AND THE ETRUSCAN RIVIERA
3. ISOLA D'ELBA
4. GROSSETO
5. PARCO NATURALE DELLA MAREMMA
6. SATURNIA
7. PITIGLIANO
8. MONTE ARGENTARIO
9. ISOLA DEL GIGLIO

• SNAPSHOT •

With fewer major routes, Southern Tuscany is more isolated than other regions and significantly less touristy. It does not, however, have a dearth of beautiful old towns. For centuries only fishermen and farmers inhabited much of the region, and it retains the appeal of an untouched country landscape. Grosseto is the only town of significant size. The sparseness of settlements means that Etruscan and Roman ruins abound (and not re-used in later eras for rebuilding). The Maremma, the area south of Piombino along the coast and inland, is a lovely hilly region with beautiful beaches and dramatic cliffs. The coastal areas have more recently become tourist destinations, with resorts and the islands of Elba and Giglio attracting wealthy Italians. You won't find much shopping here; however, the natural preserve, full of wildlife and dotted with fortress ruins, is ideal for hiking and other sports.

Massa Marittima, a mining town in the Middle Ages, retains much of its 13th-century town plan and character. Its mining history and its ancient past are reflected in the interesting museum here, while the views of the Colline Metallifere (metal-bearing hills) are anything but industrial.

Tourist Info: Ufficio Turistico *(Via Todini 3, 0566-904.756, www.grosseto.turismo.toscana.it, www.provincia.grosseto.it or www.comune.massamarittima.gr.it; call for hours)*

PLACES TO SEE
Landmarks, Arts & Entertainment:
The lower "Old Town," centered around **Piazza Garibaldi**, is medieval in style. The 11th-century **Duomo** *(Piazza Garibaldi)*, its façade composed of blind arcades, has interesting 10th-century Byzantine-style reliefs, other details from the Dark Ages, and 13th-century bas-reliefs by Giroldo da Como in the baptistery. The **Museo Archeologico** *(Palazzo del Podestà, Piazza Garibaldi, 0566-902.289, www.coopcollinemetallifere.it; hours: Apr–Oct Tu–Su 10AM–12:30PM, 3:30PM–7PM; Nov–Mar Tu–Su 10AM–12:30PM, 3PM–5PM)* has pieces from Paleolithic, Etruscan, and Roman times. The region's mining life is laid out in the **Museo della Miniera** *(Via Corridoni, 0566-902.289, www.coopcollinemetallifere.it; hours: guided tours Apr–Oct Tu–Su 10AM–5:45PM;*

Nov–Mar Tu–Su 10AM–4:30PM), part of which is in an old mine shaft.

The 14th-century "New Town," or upper town, is dominated by the Gothic Sienese Fortress and Tower, dating from the era of conflict between Pisa and Siena; Siena won out. The **Fortezza dei Senesi** (fortress) links to the **Torre del Candeliere** (tower) *(Piazza Matteotti, 0566-902.289, www.coopcollinemetallifere.it; hours: Apr–Oct Tu–Su 10AM–1PM, 3PM–6PM; Nov–Mar Tu–Su 11AM–1PM, 2:30PM–4:30PM)* via a striking arch. The **Museo di Arte e Storia delle Miniere** *(Piazza Matteotti, 0566-902.289, www.coopcollinemetallifere.it; hours: Apr–Oct Tu–Su 3PM–5:30PM; Nov–Mar by appt)* covers the ancient history and art of mining. The **Museo di Arte Sacra** *(Complesso Museale di San Pietro all'Orto, Corso Diaz 36, 0566-901.954/902.289, www.coopcolline metallifere.it; hours: Apr–Sep Tu–Su 10AM–1PM, 3PM–6PM; Oct–Mar Tu–Su 11AM–1PM, 3PM–5PM)* houses art from local churches.

PLACES TO EAT & DRINK

Get down with the locals at **Osteria da Tronca (€-€€)** *(Vicolo Porte 5, 0566-901.991; call for hours, dinner only, closed W)*, a simple, earthy eatery. **Taverna del Vecchio Borgo (€-€€)** *(Via Norma Parenti 12, 0566-903.950; hours: Tu–Su dinner, closed Feb 15–March 15)* excels in steaks, stewed wild boar, or spit-roasted pig. An old-fashioned café-bar, **Enoteca Le Logge (€)** *(Piazza Garibaldi 11, 0566-902.221; hours: winter 6AM–9PM, summer 6AM–12AM)* has great sandwiches and ice cream.

WHERE TO STAY

Hotel Il Sole (€) *(Via della Libertà 43, 0566-901.971, www.ilsolehotel.it)* is sweet and simple. Albergo Il Girifalco (€) *(Via Massetana Nord 25, 0566-902.177, www.ilgirifalco.com)* offers clean, simple rooms and lots of space near town. Tenuta Il Cicalino (€-€€) *(Loc. Cicalino 3, 0566-902.031, www.ilcicalino.it)*, six renovated farmhouses in the countryside, offers simple, beautiful rooms and exercise and spa facilities.

NEARBY PLACES TO STAY

Bivio di Caldana: The simple elegance of the rooms at Montebelli (€€-€€€) *(Molinetto area, 0566-887.100, www.montebelli.com)* reflects the beauty of the natural surroundings: hike over hills and olive groves or ride a horse through the woods.

POPULONIA AND
THE ETRUSCAN RIVIERA (2)

The Etruscan Riviera, the coastline from Livorno to Piombino, is full of pine forests, sandy beaches, and archaeological ruins. At its southern end the medieval town of Populonia, one of Italy's oldest ports, is a testament to the industriousness of the mysterious Etruscan civilization. Here they smelted iron mined on the island of Elba. The area is beautiful, with lush vegetation around the stunning, secluded Baratti Bay.

Tourist Info: Ufficio di Turismo, nearby in Piombino *(Torre Comunale, Via Ferruccio, 0565-225.639, www. turismopiombino.it)*

PLACES TO SEE
Landmarks, Arts & Entertainment:
Populonia, with its imposing fortified acropolis, sits on the hill above the small port of Baratti; the view from the battlements is breathtaking. Below the fortifications, the **Etruscan necropolis** *(www.parchivaldicornia.it; guided tours: 0565-290.02)* is an Iron Age (9th- to 8th-century B.C.) burial ground with fascinating tombs, tumuli, and chambers. The **Museo Gasparri** *(Populonia Castello, Via di Sotto 8, 0565-296.66; hours: 9AM–12:30PM, 2PM–7PM, closed M in winter)* displays objects excavated from burial chambers and other local Etruscan sites.

NEARBY PLACES TO EAT & DRINK

San Vincenzo: From chef-owner Fulvio Pierangelini's exquisite creations to the beautiful décor and table settings, everything is exceptional at **Gambero Rosso (€€€€)** *(Piazza della Vittoria 13, 0565-701.021; hours: W–Su 12:30PM–2PM, 8PM–10PM, closed Nov–Dec)*, one of Italy's finest restaurants. **Castagneto Carducci: Ristorante Da Ugo (€)** *(Via Pari 3, 0565-763.746; call for hours, closed M)* specializes in game and mushrooms; rabbit, wood pigeon, and pork are among the Maremma and Tuscan dishes served.

NEARBY PLACES TO STAY

Marina di Castagneto Carducci: Tombolo Talasso Resort *(€€€–€€€€)* *(Via del Corallo 3, 0565-745.30, www.tombolotalasso.it)* is a luxury spa with modern rooms. **San Vincenzo:** Poggio ai Santi *(€€–€€€)* *(Via San Bartolo 100, 0565-798.032, www.poggioaisanti.com)* consists of a group of converted farmhouses, serene with modern interior design and a fabulous view over a valley to the sea. **Sassetta:** Tenuta La Bandita *(€–€€€)* *(Via Campagna Nord 30, 0565-794.224, www.labandita.com)*, a converted 17th-century villa with period furniture, offers sophisticated lodgings amid orchards, olive groves, and woodlands.

ISOLA D'ELBA (3)

Italy's third largest island, Elba is a mix of mountains, olive groves, sheer cliffs, sea caves, rocky beaches, and sandy shores. Known as Napoleon's island of exile, it is a mix of wild nature and developed tourism. Its many resorts offer water sports, and the national park in the northwest (around Marciana and Poggio) is a hiker's dream.

To get there: Catch a ferry from the port of **Piombino** to Elba's capital, **Portoferraio**, run by **Toremar** *(0565-311.00 or 0565-226.590, www.toremar.it)*. You can buy tickets at the port.

Tourist Info: APT *(Portoferraio, Viale Elba 4, 0565-914.671, www.aptelba.it or www.elbaisola.it; call for hours)*

PLACES TO SEE
Landmarks, Arts & Entertainment:
In the middle of **Portoferraio** is one of Napoleon's houses, **Villa dei Mulini** *(Piazzale Napoleone, 0565-915.846; call for hours)*, now a museum, built beside two windmills. About three miles away, the emperor's country home, **Villa Napoleonica San Martino** *(San Martino, 0565-914.688; call for hours)*, has a Neoclassical façade and Egyptian-style frescoes. At **Rio Marina** the **Museo dei Minerali Elbani** *(Via Magenta 26, 0565-962.088, www.parcominelba.it; hours: 9:30AM–*

12:30PM, 3:30PM–6:30PM) is a fine mineralogical museum. When you tire of museums, take time to explore all of the island's various beaches.

PLACES TO EAT & DRINK

Portoferraio: On the seacoast, **La Barca (€-€€)** *(Via Guerrazzi 60, 0565-918.036; call for hours, closed W)* serves excellent seafood, mainly grilled. **Marciana: Osteria del Noce (€€-€€€)** *(Via della Madonna 14, 0565-901. 284, www.osteriadelnoce.it; call for hours, open mid-Mar–Sep)* serves Ligurian cuisine in a lovely setting with terrace sea views. **Rio Marina:** Elba's top restaurant, **La Canocchia (€-€€)** *(Via Palestro 2-4, 0565-962.432, www.lacanocchia.com; call for hours, closed Nov–Jan)*, does local dishes and creative seafood. **Porto Azzurro:** With harbor views, **La Lanterna Magica (€€)** *(Via Lungomare Vitaliani 5, 0565-958.394, www.ristorantela lanternamagica.it; call for hours)* is an upscale fish place.

WHERE TO STAY

Sant'Andrea: On a cliff overlooking the sea, **Da Giacomino (€)** *(Capo Sant'Andrea, 0565-908.010, www. hoteldagiacomino.it)* has simple rooms (some with terraces) and a glorious garden. **Fetovaia:** Two clean, comfortable, more upscale choices are **Hotel lo Scirocco (€-€€)** *(Via del mare, 0565-988.033, www.hotello sciroccoisolaelba.it)* and **Anna (€-€€)** *(Via del Canaletto 215/c, 0565-988.032, www.hotelannaisolaelba.it)*. **Hotel Villa Ottone (€€-€€€)** *(Loc. Ottone, 0565-933.042, www.villaottone.com)* is swanky, with beautiful rooms, palm tree-lined gardens, and a private beach.

GROSSETO (4)

Much destroyed in World War II, Grosseto still has a small historic center and 16th-century walls. It's the largest town in southern Tuscany. Although not especially charming, the town has a few worthwhile sights.

Tourist Info: APT *(Viale Monterosa 206, 0564-462.611, www.grosseto.turismo.toscana.it or www.provincia.grosseto. it; call for hours)*

PLACES TO SEE
Landmarks, Arts & Entertainment:

The **Museo Archeologico** *(Piazza Baccarini 3, 0564-488.750, www.gol.grosseto.it; hours: Mar–Apr Tu–Su 9:30AM–1PM, 4PM–6PM; May–Oct Tu–Su 10AM–1PM, 5PM–8PM; Nov–Feb Tu–F 9AM–1PM, Sa–Su 9:30AM–1PM, 4PM–6PM)* has collected many of the Etruscan and Roman artifacts from the Maremma and **Roselle**, outside Grosseto, where an important Etruscan town has been excavated. Roman sites among the ruins at **Rovine di Roselle** *(SS223, 6 miles NE of Grosseto, 0564-402.403; hours: M–Sa 8:30AM–sunset, Su 8:30AM–7:45PM)* are evidence of the swift rise of Rome at the expense of Etruria and the transience of civilizations. The digs continue at Roselle, as well as in the area of **Vetulonia**, another important excavation nearby, where an Etruscan necropolis and other sites are open to the public.

PLACES TO EAT & DRINK

Buca di San Lorenzo (€€) *(Viale Manetti 1, 0564-251.42; call for hours Tu–Sa, closed 2 wks in Jan & July)* serves fish and traditional Tuscan dishes in an elegant medieval décor. **Il Canto del Gallo** (€-€€) *(Via Mazzini 29, 0564-414.589; call for hours, M–Sa)* specializes in chicken, cold cuts, and vegetarian dishes.

NEARBY PLACES TO EAT

Seggiano: Elegant **Il Silene** (€€-€€€) *(Pescina area, north-east of Grosseto, 0564-950.805, www.ilsilene.it; hours: Tu–Su 12:45PM–2PM, 7:45PM–9:30PM, closed Su–M in winter)* offers a dining experience to delight any gourmet.

WHERE TO STAY

Within the 16th-century Medici Walls, the **Grand Hotel Bastiani** (€€) *(Piazza Gioberti 64, 0564-200.47, www.hotelbastiani.com)* is pleasant and comfortable.

NEARBY PLACES TO STAY

Campagnatico: **Villa Bellaria** (€) *(Via dei Granai 1, 0564-996.626/0577-281.716, www.villabellaria.it)*, a country home that has changed hands among noble families, has spacious bedrooms on an estate with a large park.

PARCO NATURALE DELLA MAREMMA (5)

Trails, slopes, and beaches make the Parco Naturale della Maremma, a WWF-protected nature preserve, fabulous for hiking, canoeing, and horseback riding. Birdwatching is exciting, with falcons, kingfishers, osprey, herons, storks, and even the Knight of Italy as area residents. Butterflies too are abundant, as are wild boar, lizards, poisonous snakes, and other wildlife. Cowboys *(butteri)* tend to longhorn cattle and hold rodeos. The wild, natural beach at Marina di Alberese has wide, sandy beaches below sheer cliffs.

Visitor Center: Centro Visite di Alberese *(Via Bersagliere 7-9, 0564-407.098, www.parcomaremma.it; hours: mid-June–Sep 7:30AM–10AM, 4PM–6PM; Oct–mid-June 9AM–1 hr before sunset; also, www.alberese.info and www.grosseto.turismo.toscana.it)*

PLACES TO SEE
Landmarks, Arts & Entertainment:

In the park, the Medici-built watchtowers **Torre di Castelmarino** and **Torre di Collelungo** *(near Marina di Alberese)* protected the coast from attack. Among ruins of the 12th-century abbey **Abbazia di San Rabano** *(east of Torre di Collelungo)* are a 14th-century tower and fort. At the southern tip of the park is **Talamone**, a little fishing village topped by a 15th-century fortress. Legend has it that Telamon, one of Jason's Argonauts who searched for the Golden Fleece, is buried beneath the hill above the town.

NEARBY PLACES TO EAT & DRINK

Alberese: Mancini & Caoduro (€) *(Via del Fante 24, 0564-407.137; call for hours, closed Tu & Nov–Feb)* does pizza, pasta, and cold cuts. **Alberese Scalo:** La Nuova Dispensa (€) *(Via Aurelia Vecchia 11, 0564-407.321; call for hours, closed Tu in winter)* serves local dishes; try the wild boar *cacciatore*. **Talamone:** La Buca di Nonno Ghigo (€€) *(Piazza Garibaldi 1, 0564-887.067; call for hours, closed Nov & M in winter)* is a delightful spot for fresh fish.

NEARBY PLACES TO STAY

Castiglione della Pescaia: Agriturismo La Rombaia (€-€€) *(Rombaia area, 0564-944.012, www.agriturismola rombaia.it)* provides comfort and simplicity in a tranquil setting. **Talamone:** Talamone International Camping Village (€) *(Via Talamonese, 0564-887.026, www.*

talamonecampingvillage.com) is large, affording privacy; a pool, private beach, and sports activities are on site. Hotel Il Telamonio (€-€€) *(Piazza Garibaldi 4, 0564-887.008, www.hoteliltelamonio.com)* is on a square in the old town center. **Fonteblanda:** Villa Bengodi (€€) *(Via Bengodi 2, 0335-644.5596, www.villabengodi.it)*, a charming B&B, has a lovely garden and sea views.

SATURNIA (6)

Once Etruscan, Saturnia was taken over by the Romans, who changed its name, believing the myth that Saturn launched a thunderbolt that cracked the earth in this spot, creating the hot springs that today attract so many visitors. Nearby is the town of Montemerano, a lovely, quiet, and less-touristy destination.

Tourist Info: Consorzio Turistico L'Altra Maremma *(Via Mazzini 4, 0564-601.280, www.laltramaremma.it)*

PLACES TO SEE
Landmarks, Arts & Entertainment:
Saturnia is famous for its thermal waters and spa, **Terme di Saturnia** *(0564-600.111, www.termedisaturnia.it)*. For free, you can get the effects of the hot sulphurous waters at the lovely waterfalls and pools of **Cascate del Gorello** *(Montemerano road)*. The hill town of **Montemerano**, with its flowering gardens, stone houses, and medieval castle, is a strikingly picturesque village.

PLACES TO EAT & DRINK
Bacco e Cerere (€€-€€€) *(Via Mazzini 4, 0564-601.235; call for hours)* serves excellent meat dishes. **Montemerano: Da Caino (€€€€)** *(Via della Chiesa 4, 0564-602.817; call for hours, closed W, no Th lunch)*, fast becoming a star among Italian restaurants, does local specialties with fresh ingredients.

WHERE TO STAY

Terme di Saturnia (€€€) *(Via della Follonata, 0564-600.111, www.termedisaturnia.it)* is a luxury hotel and spa, with a wellness center and golf clinic. Elegant **Villa Clodia** (€-€€) *(Via Italia 43, 0564-601.212, www.hotelvillaclodia.com)* has beautiful, well-appointed rooms; the sauna and fitness room seem carved out of a grotto. **Montemerano:** In what was once an aristocratic home, **Relais Villa Acquaviva** (€€-€€€) *(Acquaviva area, 0564-602.890, www.relaisvillaacquaviva.com)* offers elegance, beauty, and serene luxury.

Dramatic Pitigliano looks as though it is rising out of the cliffs and is one with the stone that forms its foundation and walls. The caves in the cliffs add to the sensation that nature and civilization have wrestled and neither is the victor. Labyrinthine streets wind through the town and the remains of a spectacular aqueduct, a citadel, and ramparts with breathtaking views all add to the glorious beauty of Pitigliano.

Tourist Info: *(Piazza Garibaldi 51, 0564-617.111, www.comune.pitigliano.gr.it; hours: Tu–Su 9AM–1PM, 4PM–7PM)*

PLACES TO SEE
Landmarks, Arts & Entertainment:

Vestiges of the Aldobrandeschi and Orsini families, who controlled the town through the ages, are visible, most prominently in the **Palazzo Orsini** *(Piazza Orsini, 0564-616.074; hours: summer 10AM–1PM, 4PM–7PM; winter 10AM–1PM, 3PM–5PM)*, which houses a museum. The **Museo Etrusco** *(Piazza Orsini 59, 0564-614.067; hours: Palm Sunday–early Nov M–F 10AM–1PM, 3PM–4PM, Sa–Su 10AM–1PM, 2PM–7PM; early Dec 10AM–1PM, 2PM–4PM, late Dec–early Jan 10AM–1PM, 3PM–4PM, other times by appt)* displays pieces from local excavations. The **Museo Ebraico** and Synagogue *(Vicolo Marghera & Vicolo Manin, 0564-616.006; hours: June–Sep Su–F 10AM–12:30PM, 3:30PM–6:30PM;*

Oct–Nov, Mar–May Su–F 10AM–12:30PM, 3PM–6PM; Dec–Feb Su–F 10AM–12:30PM, 3PM–5:30PM) trace the history and culture of a once thriving Jewish community that settled here in the 16th century and all but disappeared during World War II. The **Jewish Ghetto** retains the vestiges of that community: the women's ritual baths, a kosher butcher, a bakery, a cemetery, and other establishments.

PLACES TO EAT & DRINK

In a cave of the rock wall, award-winning **Il Tufo Allegro** (€€) *(Vicolo della Costituzione 5, 0564-616.192; hours: Th–M 12:30PM–2PM, 7:30PM–9:30PM, W 7:30PM–9:30PM, closed Jan 1–Feb 15 & July 1-15)* serves stupendous renditions of local favorites: chicken pâté with red onion marmalade and *vin santo* jelly, ricotta and spinach dumplings *(gnudi)* in truffle sauce, and rabbit with wild fennel. Other restaurants offering good local cuisine are: **Il Grillo** (€) *(Via Cavour 18, 0564-615.202; call for hours, closed Tu & July)* and **Dell'Orso** (€) *(Piazza San Gregorio VII 14-15, 0564-614.273; call for hours, closed Th in winter)*, where you can sit outside and enjoy the view of the piazza.

NEARBY PLACES TO STAY

Sorano: Hotel Della Fortezza (€€) *(Piazza Cairoli 5, 0564-632.010, www.hoteldellafortezza.com, closed Jan–Feb)*, a charming inn in the Orsini Fortress, has incredible views of the town and surrounding woods.

MONTE ARGENTARIO (8)

Once an island, Monte Argentario is a rugged peninsula of cliffs, coves, and bays. The harbors of **Porto Ercole** and **Porto Santo Stefano** are full of yachts—Italian politicians favor Porto Santo Stefano—during holidays while fishermen take over the piers in the off-season.

Tourist Info: Porto Santo Stefano *(Corso Umberto 55, or Archetto del Palio 1, 0564-814.208; call for hours, closed Su; www.monteargentario.it or www.provincia.grosseto.it)*

PLACES TO EAT & DRINK

Porto Ercole: Arguably the best restaurant in the area, **Osteria dei Nobili Santi** (€€-€€€) *(Via dell'Ospizio 8, 0564-833.015; hours: Tu–Sa 7:30PM–10:30PM, Su 12PM–2:30PM, 7:30PM–10:30PM)* serves divinely inspired fish dishes: octopus pâté, zucchini stuffed with pâté of sea bass, prawns in filo leaves with orange sauce, squid and *porcini* mushroom soup, or standards like spaghetti with clams. **Porto Santo Stefano: Dal Greco** (€€€) *(Via del Molo 1-2, 0564-814.885; call for hours, closed Tu & Nov–Jan)*, overlooking the harbor, is a great seafood restaurant. **Da Orlando** (€€) *(Via Breschi 3, 0564-812.788; call for hours, closed W)* also has great views and is quieter. The view from **Il Moresco** (€€) *(Via Panoramica 156, Cala Moresca, 0564-824.158 or 0330-247.308, www.ilmoresco.com; call for hours)*, up on a cliff, is breathtaking; the food is good too.

WHERE TO STAY

Porto Ercole: Harborside Hotel Don Pedro (€€) *(Via Panoramica 7, 0564-833.914, www.hoteldonpedro.it)* has fabulous sea views. Il Pellicano (€€€€) *(Sbarcatello area, 0564-858.111, www.pellicanohotel.com)*, a deluxe villa with wooden ceiling beams, antiques, and lovely views, has a private beach. **Porto Santo Stefano:** Hotel Torre di Cala Piccola (€€€) *(Cala Piccola area, 0564-825.111, www.torredicalapiccola.com)* is in a sensational spot on the cliffs overlooking the sea.

ISOLA DEL GIGLIO (9)

Isola del Giglio is a small, picturesque island with great beaches. There are three villages: **Giglio Porto**, where the ferry arrives; **Giglio Campese**, the main beach; and **Giglio Castello**, a medieval village. Other small beaches dot the coastline.

To get there: Catch a boat from Porto Santo Stefano to Giglio. Boats are run by **Toremar** *(0564-810.803/ 818.455, www.toremar.it)* and **Maregiglio** *(0564-812. 920, www.maregiglio.it)*. Buy tickets at the port.

Tourist Info: Pro Loco *(Via Provinciale 9, 0564-809.400, www.isoladelgigliouofficioturistico.com or www.isoladel giglio.it; hours: Easter–Oct 9AM–12:30PM, 4PM–6PM)*

PLACES TO EAT & DRINK

Giglio Porto: **La Margherita** *(€) (Via Thaon de Revel 5, 0564-809.237; call for hours, Easter–Sep, Tu–Su)* serves good fish dishes; try the *cavatelli con mazzancolle e pecorino (pasta with mantis shrimp and pecorino cheese)*. **Giglio Castello:** Up in the hills with a view of the sea, **Trattoria Da Maria** *(€€-€€€) (Via della Casa Matta 12, 0564-806.062, www.ristorantedamaria.it; call for hours, Mar–Dec, Th–Tu)* serves fish, meat, and the local special-ty, rabbit. Fresh fish at **Da Santi** *(€-€€) (Via Marconi 20, 0564-806.188; call for hours, closed M in winter)* mixes beautifully with local vegetables. **Giglio Campese:** On the long, sandy beach, **Tony's** *(€€) (Via della Torre 13, 0564-806.453; call for hours)* is dependable for drinks and food.

WHERE TO STAY

Giglio Porto: In a fabulous panoramic spot overlooking the sea, Hotel Castello Monticello (€-€€) *(Via Provinciale, 0564-809.252, www.hotelcastellomonticello.com; closed Nov–Feb)* has all the amenities of a deluxe hotel. Hotel Bahamas (€) *(Via Cardinale Oreglia 22, 0564-809.254, www.bahamashotel.it)* offers simple, spare rooms. Secluded, accessible only by foot or boat, Pardini's Hermitage (€€€) *(Cala degli Alberi area, 0564-809.034, www.hermit.it, closed mid-Oct–late Apr)* is the perfect seaside retreat.

Open my heart and you will see,
graved inside of it, "Italy."

—*Robert Browning*

INDEX

232

NOTES

NOTES

NOTES

NOTES